General Principles of Korean Commercial Law

KI JONG LEE

Professor, College of Law and Director, Institute for Legal Studies, Sookmyung Women's University, Korea

SAM YOUNG SA

General Principles of
Korean Commercial Law

Published by SAM YOUNG SA. 335, Achasan-ro, Gwangjin-gu,
Seoul, Republic of Korea.
October 26, 2020

ISBN 978-89-445-0518-8-93360
Price ₩17,000
Printed in Korea

PREFACE

Foreigners' attention to Korean commercial law has increased rapidly, as Korea became one of the top 10 economies in the world and has adopted the open market economy, allowing foreign direct investment and negotiating FTA's with numerous countries. The growing interest in Korean commercial law has led to an increasing number of publications on the subject, written in English language.

Most of the early publications were practical guides for doing business in Korea, covering a wide range of laws and regulations concerning businesses.[1)] They were valuable materials for practitioners when there were only a few resources on Korean law readily available in English.[2)] However, they could not go deeper into each area of law, due to the limitation of space.

Later, more focused volumes on individual areas of Korean commercial law have been published. The most popular topic was company law,[3)] although recently publishers are seeking more diversity in their publications, going into other areas, such as insurance law and transport law.[4)]

However, publishers' attention has not yet reached one of the most fundamental topics of Korean commercial law: the general principles of commercial law. These principles apply to all the commercial transactions (*e.g.* insurance contract) and business organizations (*e.g.* companies). All the other topics of commercial law are based on the foundations of those principles. Thus the principles are the bare essentials in a systemetic research of Korean commercial law.

This volume focuses on those general principles of Korean commercial law. Its main objective is to introduce foreign researchers and practitioners to the fundamental concepts and principles of Korean commercial law. It does not try to deal with all the issues on the topic. Rather it endeavors to portray the theoretical framework of the topic and provide plentiful examples of how those principles appy to each area of commercial law, especially in Part II, entitled "The Special Characteristics of Commercial Law." I hope the volume could be an introductory material for the scholars and practitioners who are interested in a systemetic research of Korean commercial law.[5)]

October 2020

Ki Jong Lee

CONTENTS

PART I
INTRODUCTION

PART II
SPECIAL FEATURES OF COMMERCIAL LAW

PART Ⅲ
GENERAL PROVISIONS

PART I

INTRODUCTION

CHAPTER Ⅰ
WHAT IS COMMERCIAL LAW?

As an introduction I'd like to first talk about the definition of commercial law, and then look at two cases that illustrate a difference between commercial law and civil law.

Ⅰ. DEFINITION OF COMMERCIAL LAW

The term "commercial law', or *sang-bop* in Korean, has two different meanings in Korea: commercial law in a narrow sense and commercial law in a broad sense.

Commercial law "in a narrow sense" indicates a specific statute, entitled "the Commercial Act." It is a fundamental statute of Korean commercial law. The Act was first enacted by the legislature in 1962 as Act No. 1000, and has been amended several times since then. The current version is Act No. 17362, which was amended on June 9, 2020.

Commercial law "in a broad sense" includes not only the

Commercial Act, but also all the laws concerning business enterprises.[6] The most remarkable statues that belong to commercial law include:

- Financial Investment Services and Capital Market Act ("Capital Market Act" for Short)
- Monopoly Regulation and Fair Trade Act ("Fair Trade Act" for short)
- Framework Act on Consumers

But the list of commercial law statues goes on and on. It seems almost open-ended, as new statutes are constantly being added. But you don't have to worry. We will focus only on the Commercial Act, that is, commercial law in a narrow sense.

The Commercial Act has 6 parts as follows: Part I General Provisions; Part II Commercial Activities; Part III Companies; Part IV Insurances; Part V Maritime Commerce; and Part VI Air Transport.

In this volume we will mainly deal with the first two parts of the Act: "General Provisions" and "Commercial Activities", which are taught in Korean universities under the title of "General Principles of Commercial Law." The "General Provisions" part contains chapters on the coverage of the act, merchants, commercial employees, trade names, trade books, commercial registry and the transfer of business. The "Commercial Activities" part contains a chapter on common provisions which apply to all the merchants regardless of their types of businesses, and several other chapters on various types of commercial activities.

However, this book will also present you multiple examples on how the principles prescribed in the first two parts of the Commercial Act apply to other areas of commercial law, especially in Part II of the book, entitled, "Special Characteristics of Commercial Law."

Ⅱ. STRUCTURE OF STATUTES AND ARTICLES

Before we move on, let us quickly look at the general structure of Korean statutes and the structure of articles in a statute.

All the Korean statutes have the same hierarchical structurc. At the top they have parts, or *pyon* in Korean. Below a part, they have chapters, or *jang* in Korean. And chapters have sections, in Korean *jol*, and sections have subsections, in Korea *gwan*. Articles in a statute have a similar hierarchical structure. Articles, *jo* in Korean, have paragraphs, *hang* in Korean; paragraphs have subparagraphs, *ho* in Korean; and subparagraphs have items, *mok* in Korean.

Please get acquainted with these hierarchies: *pyon, jang, jol, gwan* of a statute; and *jo, hang, ho, mok* of an article in a statute.

Ⅲ. TEXTS OF STATUTES IN ENGLISH LANGUAGE

The texts of Korean statutes in English language are available at the joint website of Korea Legislation Research Institute and Korea Law Translation Center.[7] At the website you could easily search the texts of two major statutes, the Commercial Act and the Civil Act which are frequently quoted throughout this volume. However, please note that the texts available at the website are not the interpretation of the latest versions of statutes.[8]

CHAPTER II
COMMERCIAL LAW V. CIVIL LAW

Here I'd like to present you two cases, involving similar transactions. These cases will help you to understand the difference between commercial law and civil law, or *min-bop* in Korean, which deals with private lives of citizens, concerning properties and families. These cases will help you understand the special features, the special characteristics, of commercial law, by revealing the contrast between the civil law principles and the commercial law principles. The cases are very simple.

[CASE 1] Amy had always wanted to have a pet dog. To be more specific, she wanted a "cup dog," a tiny Maltese. One of her neighbors had a Maltese, and it recently gave birth to babies. Amy asked the neighbor to sell one of the babies to her. The neighbor readily consented. Amy bought the dog for KRW 100,000. The baby dog grew fast, so fast that, in a few weeks, she could not contain the dog in a "cup." Further, in a few more weeks, the dog grew so big that she could not contain the dog even in a big pot. Now, after two weeks have passed from the date of sale, Amy has to admit that the dog is everything but a "cup" dog. In other words, it was not the kind of dog that she had intended to buy. Here goes our question for Case 1: "Could Amy cancel the transaction?"

[CASE 2] Ms. Simpson is a pet shop owner. She placed an order with a wholesaler for a "cup" dog. A small baby dog was delivered to her, and she paid KRW 70,000 for it. Unfortunately, the dog grew at exactly the same speed as the dog that Amy bought in Case 1. After two weeks from the date of sale, Ms. Simpson found that the dog is not the kind she had ordered. Here goes our question for Case 2, which is virtually the same as that for Case 1: "Could Ms. Simpson cancel the transaction?"

Ⅰ. ISSUES

Both of these cases involve the same type of transactions: sales, or *mae-mae* in Korean. One of the parties gives a stuff to the other party, and the other party pays for it. A stuff comes in, and money goes out: that's a sale. The Civil Act, which deals with citizens' private lives concerning properties, contains provisions on sales. On the other hand, and at the same time, the Commercial Act, which deals with business enterprises, also has provisions on sales. And the content of those provisions in the two statutes are quite different from each other. Our two cases reveal one of the most distinct differences between commercial law and civil law.

Ⅱ. WARRANTY AGAINST DEFECTS

In the two cases that we just saw, each buyer found that the dog she had purchased has some defects: it were not the kind that she originally wanted. In such a situation, both the Commercial Act and the Civil Act demand the seller to remedy the defect. We call this particular responsibility of a seller, "warranty against defects," or *ha-ja-dam-bo-chaeg-im* in Korean. But the commercial law principles on the issue is quite different from the civil law principles. The remedies themselves are similar under those two Acts. That is, both of the Acts provide for similar remedies for the buyer in case of defects. However, the Commercial Act imposes much harsher conditions on the buyer than the Civil Act. So, in order to resolve our questions, we have to first decide which one of those two statutes shall apply to each case.

The Civil Act has several general provisions on sales. And the Commercial Act has only a few special provisions on sales concerning some specific issues, such as warranty against defects that we are now dealing with.[9] The special provisions in the Commercial Act provisions on sales shall apply only to a sale between merchants, where both of the parties are merchants. They do not apply to a sale between non-merchants or a sale between a merchant and a non-merchant. If any one of the parties to the sale is a non-merchant, then the general provisions in the Civil Act shall apply.

In Case 1, the sale was made between neighbors, that is, non-merchants. Of course, Amy or her neighbor could be a merchant at their workplaces. But as long as they made the sale in their capacity as non-merchant, it's a sale between non-merchants. So the Civil Act provisions shall apply to the transaction. Whereas, in Case 2, both of the parties are merchants: a pet shop owner and a wholesaler. So the Commercial Act provisions on sales shall apply to the transaction.

Now let's look into the differences between the conditions for remedies under the Civil Act and those under the Commercial Act. First, the Civil Act provides for various types of remedies, when a buyer purchase a stuff with a defect: (i) the buyer can cancel the transaction; (ii) she can claim damages against the seller; and (iii) she can demand a stuff without a defect.[10] And the buyer shall exercise the rights to these remedies within 6 months after she found out the defect.[11] Thus, in Case 1, Amy can cancel the transaction, because, obviously, it has not been 6 months after she found out the defect: only two weeks have passed from the date of sale.

The Commercial Act provides for similar remedies for a buyer who bought a stuff with a defect. But the conditions for such remedies are much stricter under Commercial Act than under the Civil Act. The Commercial Act Article 69(1) says that the buyer should immediately examine the item when she received it and notify the seller of the defect instantly. If the buyer fails to meet these requirements, she can neither cancel the transaction, nor demand a reduction in the price, nor claim damages. She cannot pursue any of these remedies. That's the principle.

However, there are two exceptions for this principle. *First,* if the defect was not immediately discoverable, the buyer can have the second chance. To be more precise, if it was practically impossible to find out the defect right after the buyer received it, and the buyer found out the defect within 6 months, she can cancel the transaction. For example, if it is hard even for an expert to distinguish a purebred Maltese from a crossbred when it is a baby (I don't know if it is true or not), then it can be a defect which is "not immediately discoverable." *Second*, if the seller acted in bad faith, in other words, if she already knew of the defect, the provision, the principle, shall not apply. So the buyer can cancel the transaction, even if she failed to examine the stuff immediately.

Here, I'd like to encourage you to read the original text of the article, so that you could get accustomed to its original wording.

Here is the text of the article with a little bit of annotation.

> Article 69 (Buyer's Duty to Examine Subject-Matter and to Notify Defects therein)
>
> (1) *[The first sentence talks about the principle.]* In cases of a sale between merchants, the buyer shall, upon receipt of the subject matter, inspect it without delay, and immediately give a notice thereof to the seller if any defect or deficiency in numbers is found therein; otherwise, he/she has no right to rescind the contract, to demand price cuts or to claim damages thereby. *[The next sentence talks about an exception.]* The same shall apply in cases where, within six months, the buyer discovers in the subject matter of the sale a defect which was not immediately discoverable.
>
> (2) *[This paragraph talks about another exception.]* The provisions of the preceding paragraph shall not apply to the seller acting in bad faith.

Thus, in Case 2, Ms. Simpson can cancel the transaction, only if she immediately examine the baby dog and notify the wholesaler of the defect. Unfortunately, however, she belatedly found out the defect after two weeks have passed from the date of sale. So, in principle, she cannot cancel the transaction. I said "in principle," because, as we just saw, there are two exceptions: *first*, if the defect was not "immediately discoverable", as the original text of the Act puts it, Ms. Simpson can cancel the transaction; *second*, if the wholesaler "acted in bad faith", she can still cancel the transaction.

Ⅲ. LAW FOR PROFESSIONALS V. LAW FOR AMATEURS

At this point, you might get quite curious. "Why do the two statutes, the Commercial Act and the Civil Act, say so differently on the same matter?" The answer has something to do with the coverage of the two statutes. As we saw earlier[12)], the Commercial Act provisions on sales apply to sales involving only merchants, while the Civil Act provisions apply to sales involving at least one non-merchant party.

Here let me give you another sports analogy. Merchants are like professional players, while non-merchants are like amateurs. Harsher rules apply to professionals in sports games. For example, amateur boxers wear helmets, while professionals do not. Gloves are thicker in amateur boxing matches than in professional matches. All these measures are designed to protect the amateur players. But the professionals have to protect themselves with their own skills and techniques.

Likewise, in sales involving a non-merchant party, the law, the Civil Act, protects the non-merchant, or the amateur, by allowing several months to examine the stuff that she bought. But in sales involving merchants only, the law, the Commercial Act, places a greater emphasis on the swiftness of transaction than on the protection of buyers. Under the Commercial Act, the merchant-buyer, or the professional, has to protect themselves by immediately examining the stuff. It's like saying that: "You received a stuff, and you did not appeal at once. Now the seller is busy to deal with other new transactions. Don't' call him anymore! You are history!" Later we will see in some more details how the Commercial Act promotes the swiftness of transaction to help merchants make more profit[13)].

This *professional-amateur* analogy is very useful in understanding the differences between the Civil Act and the Commercial Act. The Civil Act principles can be compared to rules for amateurs, while the Commercial Act principles can be compared to rules for professionals[14)]. We will further build on this analogy, when we compare these two Acts on a broader basis later. But, at the moment, just bear in your mind that the commercial law is like a law for professionals, while the civil law is like a law for amateurs.

PART II

SPECIAL FEATURES OF COMMERCIAL LAW

CHAPTER Ⅰ
OPERATIONAL FEATURES

Ⅰ. PROFIT-MAKING

In the previous chapter, we saw that the Commercial Act contains some rules for merchants that are harsher than the rules for non-merchants under the Civil Act. Drawing a sports analogy, we compared the Commercial Act to the rules for professionals, while we compared the Civil Act to the rules for amateurs. Let's build some more on this analogy to understand the special characteristics of commercial law.

What is the most outstanding difference between professionals and amateurs? Skills, equipment, fame *etc.* might come into your minds. But one of the most fundamental features of professionals shall be the fact that they earn money, sometimes a big amount of money, for their plays. Of course, money is not the only motivation for professional players. But it is quite a distinguishing feature of professionals, especially when we compare them to amateurs.

Back to our topic, money is one of the main themes of

commercial law. As a law for professionals, the commercial law wants to help professionals, or merchants, to make as much money as possible. In other words, the commercial law promotes profit-making by merchants. This "profit-making" feature is definitely the most prominent and special characteristics of commercial law. All the other features of commercial law, that we will survey later, stem from this fundamental, profit-making feature of commercial law. People often say that there is no such thing as free lunch. But, in a commercial world, "Indeed, there is no free lunch with a merchant!"

Let's look at some examples of how the commercial law promotes profit-making by merchants.

Suppose that you need to pay tuition by the end of this week, but temporarily you don't have sufficient funds. Your funds will be restored in a few weeks. So you decide to borrow some money from your neighbor, promising that you will repay the loan in a month. After a month, your funds are restored, and you pay the money back to your neighbor with gratitude. Here goes a question. "Should you pay the *interest* for the loan to your neighbor?"

If you have promised to pay the interest, you will certainly have to pay the interest. But, what if you and your neighbor have never agreed on it? When there is no agreement at all on the payment of interest, do you still have to pay it? It's a very interesting question.

I hope all of you could think about it for a minute. Do you have to pay the interest, even when you and your creditor have never mentioned it? The answer can be found in the Civil Act. The transaction in this case is called "loan for consumption," or *so-bi-dae-cha* in Korean, under the Act Article 598. When you loan some money for consumption, you borrow money, spend it, and repay the same amount to your creditor. You don't have to return the same bank notes that you originally received from the creditor. You need only to pay the same amount of money back to her. That's why we call it loan for "consumption." On the other hand when you get a "loan for use," or *sa-yong-dae-cha* in Korean, of a stuff, say a bicycle, then you have to return the very stuff, the very bicycle, which you originally received (Civil Act Article 609).

Anyway, under the Civil Act, the lender cannot claim interest against the borrower, unless otherwise agreed. In other words, you don't have to pay the interest for a loan, as long as you and your creditor did not agree on it. It is a generous rule for the debtor, but it allows only a narrow chance for the creditor to gain profit from the loan.

However, when we turn to a commercial transaction, the atmosphere changes drastically. The Commercial Act Article 55(1) says, "When a merchant has loaned money to another person in respect of his/her business, the merchant may claim statutory interest." It means that you have to pay the interest, if you loan some money from a merchant in the course of his/her business, even if you and your creditor did not agree on interest.

When compared to the civil law principles, the commercial law principles are much harsher to the debtor, and much more favorable to the creditor. Why? Because the commercial law wants to promote profit-making by merchants. The commercial law guarantees the payment of interest to a merchant-creditor, if he/she lends some money in the course of his/her business. Here goes a commercial law catch phrase. "There is no free lunch with a merchant!" If we borrow some money from a merchant, we have to pay the price of her money, *i.e.* the interest, even if there is no agreement on it.

That's not all. Please read more carefully te article 55(1) of the Commercial Act. It says that a debtor has to pay "statutory" interest. What is statutory interest? There are two types of interest: agreed interest and statutory interest. Agreed interest means an interest that the parties of a loan agreed on. For example, if the debtor agreed with the creditor to pay an interest of 7% a year, that's agreed interest. But if the parties agreed on the payment of interest, without determining the interest rate, then the debtor has to pay statutory interest.

Under the Civil Act, the statutory interest rate is 5% a year. What about the Commercial Act? Which do you think is higher, the statutory interest rate under the Civil Act or that under the Commercial Act? Yes, you are right. The statutory interest rate is higher under the Commercial Act. It's 6% a year.

Why? Because the Commercial Act wants to promote profit-making by merchants. It guarantees higher rate of statutory interest, in case of the absence of the agreement on interest rate. So if you borrow some money from a merchant, and agree to pay the interest, without fixing the interest rate, the statutory interest rate of 6% a year applies. Further, if you borrow some money from a merchant, without agreeing on the interest at all, you still have to pay the statutory interest of 6% a year. I mean, suppose you did not agree on the payment of interest in the first place, not to mention the interest rate. Even in that case, you still have to pay the statutory interest of 6% a year under the Commercial Act. Here goes another commercial law catch phrase. "There is no *cheap* lunch with a merchant!"

Let's look at another example. The Commercial Act Article 55(2) says, "If a merchant has made substituted donation for another person within the scope of his/her business, the merchant may request for statutory interest thereon from the date of the substituted donation." "Substituted donation" here means a payment of money on behalf of another person. For example, suppose that you are a carrier, *i.e.* a merchant, and you paid the insurance cost for a package on behalf of your client. That's a payment on behalf of other person, *i.e.* substituted donation. As the payment was made within the scope of your business, you can not only demand the reimbursement of the insurance cost itself, but also the payment of its statutory interest, which is 6% a year under the Commercial Act.

One last example. Suppose that you found your neighbor's dog at the doorstep. The dog is starving and sick. Your neighbor was away from home, traveling abroad, and the dog somehow got out of the house and could not go back in. You took care of the dog, providing food and medicine. You did it without any legal duty, and it is called "management of affairs" or *sa-moo-gwan-ri* in Korean under the Civil Act Article 734. In case of management of affairs without any legal duty, the manager can demand the reimbursement of expenses (Civil Act Article 739). So when your neighbor returns home, you could demand her to repay the cost of food and medicine. But, under the Civil Act, you cannot claim for the price of your effort. You can claim for the compensation for the cost, but not for your effort.

As you might already anticipate, the commercial law says quite differently on the same matter. The Commercial Act Article 61 says, "A merchant who has performed any act on behalf of another person within the scope of his/her business may demand reasonable remunerations in respect of such an act." For example, if a hotel takes care of a dog of its client, while she is attending a conference for a few days, the hotel can claim more than the payment of the cost incurred by taking care of the dog. The hotel can also claim the statutory interest on the cost under Article 55(2) of the Commercial Act. Furthermore, the hotel can claim for the compensation for its effort in taking care of the dog under Article 61 of the Act.

The case reminds me of an old joke on lawyers. A person called her lawyer friend for legal advice. The friend gave her a detailed advice in all sincerity. She was touched by the kindness of her friend, and expressed her deep gratitude before hang up. A few days later, she received a bill from the lawyer claiming the fee for consultation. We could replace the lawyer here with a merchant: if a merchant does something within the scope of her business, she can claim the reward for her effort. Yes, indeed, "There is no *free* lunch with a merchant!"

Ⅱ. SWIFTNESS OF TRANSACTIONS

The Commercial Act provides for measures to promote profit-making by merchants, way beyond the guarantee for payment of interest and compensation for their efforts.

Suppose that there is some limit to the amount of profit that one can get from a single deal. In that case, how could she increase the total amount of profit from her overall business? The answer is obvious. She could increase the overall profit by increasing the number of transactions she makes. In order to do that, she needs to move faster. The discipline of business administration tells us much about how to increase the efficiency in businesses. But the Commercial Act, which wants to promote profit-making by merchants, also provides various measures to increase the *pace* of transactions. These measures can be classified into two groups: promoting simplicity and standardization.

A. Promoting Simplicity

Let's look at the structure of an agency relationship to understand how the Commercial Act promotes simplicity of transactions. I assume that you are quite acquainted with how the agency relationship works, even if you don't know the exact terms. Suppose that you are very busy and cannot make a deal yourself. In that case you can appoint an agent, in Korean *dae-ri-in*, and have her negotiate with the other party on behalf of yourself. Under the Civil Act you are called a principal, or *bon-in* in Korean. As the agent was given the agency power, in Korean *dae-ri-gwon*, she can make a deal on behalf of yourself. However, in order to make it clear that you are the party to the contract, not the agent, the agent should disclose the fact that she is acting on behalf of the principal, *i.e.* yourself. For example, when an agent signs a contract, she shall set forth her capacity as an agent, by stating "on behalf of (the principal)" or "as the agent of (the principal)" or something like that. That's what the Civil Act Article 114(1) demands.

However, if you appoint an agent for *business* transactions, the disclosure of agency relationship could either be burdensome, or even redundant or unnecessary. For instance, suppose that you visit a shop and look for a stuff. Someone at the shop approaches you to recommend a brand. You ask some questions to her, negotiate the price with her, and finally make a deal: you bought a stuff from her. But later she turns out to be a clerk, and the shop owner claim the deal is void. Do you think the contract shall be annulled on the ground that the clerk did not state that she is not a principal, but just an agent? Of course, not. We buy stuffs every day, and hardly care if the person we negotiate with is the shop owner or just a clerk. If the law says that all those deals should be annulled unless the agent, i.e. the clerk, states her capacity as agent, it will bring about unnecessary burden both on the client and the merchant. So, unlike the Civil Act, the Commercial Act does not require a disclosure of agency relationship in commercial transactions. The main sentence of the Commercial Act Article 48 says, "A commercial activity conducted by an agent shall be effective toward the principal, even if the agent does not indicate that he or she is acting on behalf of the principal." So the shop owner may *not* nullify the sales contract, simply because the clerk did not tell you that she is just an agent.

B. Standardization

When we try to get a deal through, most of the time is spent for negotiation. Signing the contract itself takes only a few minutes. So if we could reduce or even eliminate the time to spend for negotiation, we could dramatically increase the pace of transactions. How do we do that? Standardization is one of the ways. By standardizing the terms of a contract, we could minimize the need for negotiation. So standardized contracts are widely used in many areas, such as transportation, banking and insurance, where companies need to deal with a large number of customers.

Standardized contract, or *yak-gwan* in Korean, has some merits: (i) it promotes efficiency in transaction; (ii) clients can benefit from the expertise of the companies in laying down the term for the contract. But it also has several demerits: (i) the terms of the contract are devised out by the merchants alone; and (ii) the consequence of this one-sidedness could be unfair clauses in the contract. So the legislature enacted a special statute to prevent the harmful consequences of standardized contract: the Regulation of Standardized Contract Act, or *yak-gwan-gyu-je-bop* in Korean. The

Act is one of the many statutes in the area of commercial law.

Ⅲ. DISREGARD OF PERSONALITY

We have been looking at the special features of commercial law, especially in comparison to civil law. We first looked at the "profit-making" feature. And then looked into how the commercial law promotes the swiftness of transactions. Now let's turn to the third feature of commercial law: disregard of personality. Let me give you a couple of examples.

A. Agents' Duty to Fulfill Contractual Obligations

In the previous chapter, we saw that an agent does not have to tell the client that she is just an agent, not the principal. Even without the statement, the principal shall be bound by the contract that the agent concluded on behalf of her.

But, what if the client does not want to deal with the principal? What if she believed that the person, who she was dealing with, was a principal rather than an agent? For instance, the agent was a trustworthy person and you made a deal with her, believing that she is the principal who shall fulfill the contract. But later you find that you are in a contractual relationship with other person, *i.e.* the principal who is not at all trustworthy. In that case your anticipation that the agent will fulfill the contract need to be satisfied, as you had no idea that you are dealing with an unreliable person. The proviso[15)] of Article 48 of the Commercial act provides a solution for the problem. It says, "Provided, That when the other party was not aware that the commercial activity was performed for the principal, such other party may also demand performance from the agent."

It doesn't mean that the agent becomes a party to the contract. The principal is still the party. The law is simply saying that the agent should fulfill the contract, if the client demands it. Here the focus is placed on who should pay or who should fulfill the contract, rather than who is the party to the contract. So, in this case, we could say that the commercial law puts payment or fulfillment of a contract above the identity of a party to it. We call this feature of commercial law, "disregard of personality."

B. Promoters' Warrant Liability for Payment

A corporation or a stock company, in Korean *joo-sik-hoe-sa*, is the most popular type of business organization in Korea. The Commercial Act provides for two methods of establishment of a corporation: (i) establishment by promoters only; and (ii) establishment by subscription. In case of the former, only the promoters invest in the company, and the procedure is simple. But in case of the latter, not only the promoters but also other people invest in the company, and the procedure is more complex: (i) promoters acquire their shares; (ii) other investors subscribe for shares; (iii) promoters allot shares among the investors; and (iv) investors pay the subscription price.

A serious problem can arise after finishing the procedure for the establishment by subscription. If it turned out that some investors failed to pay the subscription price, the company should suffer vacancy in their capital. Thus the Commercial Act Article 321 requires the promoters to pay the subscription price on behalf of those investors. We call this particular responsibility of the promoters, "promoters' warranty liability for payment." Here the original debtors, or the original obligators, are the "other" investors. But the Commercial Act does not care much about who the original debtors are. The Act focuses more on the payment, as the company cannot go on with a vacancy in its capital. Again the commercial law puts more emphasis upon the payment or the fulfillment of contract rather than the identity of the debtor. So the promoters' warranty liability for payment is another example of the disregard-of-personality feature of commercial law.

Ⅳ. FREEDOM OF CONTRACT

Now let's move on to another special feature of commercial law: freedom of contract. The freedom of contract opens a door for merchants to new opportunities for profit-making. If it were not for the freedom of contract, merchants could neither develop a new business model nor negotiate for better terms of trade. Thus the freedom of contract was originally developed as a general principle in the area of commercial law. But, the application of the principle was extended farther into the area of civil law, as the general public demanded for more and more economic freedom. Nowadays the freedom of contract is recognized as a general principle of civil law as well as commercial law. However, it should be noted here that the principle is more thoroughly applied in the area of commercial law than in the area of civil law.

Before we compare the examples of the freedom of contract under commercial law and civil law, I hope you could first understand how security or guarantee works in a creditor-debtor relationship. Suppose that *A* wants to borrow some money from *B*. If *B* is not quite sure about *A*'s credibility, *B* might hesitate to loan money to *A*. In that case, in order to reassure *B*, *A* might have to provide some "guarantee" or "security," in Korean *dam-bo*. The guarantees or securities available under Korean law can be classified into two categories: personal security and real security.

First, personal security includes guarantor or surety, in Korean *bo-jung-in*.[16] A guarantor repays the loan on behalf the original debtor, if the latter cannot pay the money back. *Second*, real security includes pledge, *jil-gwon* in Korean,[17] and mortgage, *jo-dang-gwon* in Korean.[18] A pledge is established on movable property, *dong-san* in Korean, and property rights. A mortgage is held on real estate, *boo-dong-san* in Korean, and other assets, such as cars, that shall be registered on public registry. Suppose that a creditor holds a laptop in pledge or a house on mortgage. If the debtor fails to make the payment at the stipulated time, the creditor may sell the property to get her money back in preference to other creditors. That's how the real security works.

Now let's look at pledge more closely. A pledgee, or *jil-gwon-ja* in Korean, is a creditor who holds a movable property in pledge. In this case we call the debtor a pledger, in Korean *jil-gwon-sol-jong-ja*. When the pledger cannot repay the money at a stipulated time, the pledgee may dispose of the property in two ways under Article 338 of the Civil Act: (i) she may sell the property by auction and get her money back out of the auction price in preference to other creditors; (ii) she may acquire the pledged stuff with an approval by the court. Sometimes a pledgee, *i.e.* a creditor, might want to acquire the pledged stuff without the court's approval. The debtor may allow it "after" the debt becomes due. But she may *not* allow it in advance, *i.e.* before the time for payment. The advance agreement by the debtor to allow the creditor to acquire the pledged stuff without court's approval is called "forfeited pledge," or *yoo-jil-gye-yak* in Korean. The Civil Act Article 339 prohibits such an agreement, as it could force a poverty-stricken debtor to run into a danger of losing her property to get an urgent loan.

However, the Commercial Act does *not* prohibit such an agreement, *i.e.* forfeited pledge, if the debt was borne in a commercial transaction. Article 59 of the Act says, "The provisions of Article 339 of the Civil Act shall not apply to pledges established for the purpose of securing claims arising out of commercial activities." Why? The reason is twofold. *First*, a merchant is considered to be capable of protecting herself in an economic activity. *Second*, if a merchant urgently needs a loan even by a forfeited pledge, the law should not get in the way, because a merchant cannot run a business without timely funding.

Thus, the Commercial Act reinforces the freedom of contract by eliminating the ban on forfeited pledge under the Civil Act. In doing so, the Commercial Act allows more room for the merchants to pursue their business opportunities.

V. SAFETY OF TRANSACTIONS

Earlier we saw that the Commercial Act provides for various measures to increase the pace of transaction, as the swiftness of transaction can help merchants to make more profit[19]. However, a merchant cannot increase the pace of transaction, if there is no guarantee for *safety*. Let me draw an analogy of driving a car here. Suppose that you have a super car which has a top speed of 150 mph. But you are driving on a local road. You cannot run faster than 40 mph, because you frequently encounter with signals, speed bumps, bikes, pedestrians and even handcarts moving slower than a pedestrian. If you try to speed up, you must take a great risk of accidents. So you should drive your super car at the same speed as that of a compact car. But if you enter an express way, say an autobahn, the landscape changes entirely. No signals, no speed bumps, no bikes, no pedestrians. You can accelerate the vehicle way over 40 mph. If the express way has no speed limit, you could reach the top speed of your *Bucephalas*.

Likewise, a merchant cannot pursue the swiftness of transactions, if there is no guarantee of safety in those transactions. Thus the Commercial Act provides for various measures to guarantee the safety of transactions. We could classify those measures into three groups as follows: (i) public notice, (ii) the respect for outward appearance, and (iii) strict liability. Let's look into them one by one.

A. Public Notice

Back to the driving analogy. One of the measures to guarantee the safety of driving is road signs. They show the names of streets, directions, turns, speed limits and prohibited activities. By informing the drivers of important road conditions, the road signs substantially contribute to the safety of driving. And if we enter an express way, the road signs get more intensive. They show additional information, such as lamps and interchanges. And, even if they show the same information as the road signs on a local road, they do that much more prominently. The road signs on an express way are much bigger, and they appear much more frequently. If the signs are small and appear only once or twice, drivers might miss it in their fast moving vehicles.

Likewise, both the Civil Act and the Commercial Act provide for measures to inform people of important conditions for transactions. We call these measures "public notice," in Korean *gong-si*. For example, the Civil Act provides for real estate registration, in Korean *boo-dong-san-dung-gi*. The registry contains information on the details of a particular property, its owner, mortgage holder and so on. By checking the registry, people can avoid the danger of dealing with a swindler or buying a property with defects.

The public registry system gets more intensive under the Commercial Act, as the Act has to guarantee the safety of transactions that are taking place much more rapidly and in volume. Thus the Commercial Act provides for the commercial registration, *sang-op-dung-gi* in Korean, which displays various information on the competence and financial status of merchants and the capacity of their assistants. For example, a representative director, in Korean *dae-pyo-i-sa*, of a corporation has the authority to represent the company. If he concludes a contract on behalf of the company, the company shall fulfill the contract. When we deal with a corporation, we often need information on the representative director of the company. Thus the Commercial Act Article 317(2)(ix) says that the name, residence registration number, in Korean *joo-min-dung-rok-bon-ho*, and address of a representative director shall be registered on the commercial registry.

B. Respect for Outward Appearance

We just saw that a corporation has to register the information on its representative director. However, is it really feasible to check the commercial registry whenever we deal with a corporation? What if we fail to check the registry before concluding a contract with a corporation? Let's take a look at an examlary case here to answer those questions.

> **[CASE]** *A* negotiated with *X* from a corporation *B*. *X* showed a business card, displaying her position as managing director of the company. Believing that *X* is truly a representative director of the company, *A* concluded a contract with her. *X* signed the contract as representative director of the company. But later when *A* requested the company *B* for the fulfillment of the contract, *B* rejected *A*'s request on the ground that *X* was *not* its representative director. So *A* checked the commercial registry only to find out that *X* really was not a representative director. Here goes the question. "Could *A* claim against the company *B* to fulfill the contract?"

If merchants always have to investigate into the truth before going into a contract, they cannot swiftly make the deal through. And the delay shall be a huge obstacle to profit-making by merchants. Thus the Commercial Act has several provisions to protect a party to a transaction by applying the principle of the respect for outward appearance.[20] The principle says that when its three requirements are met, an outward appearance shall be respected as if it is a fact. Those three requirements are: (i) appearance, (ii) imputation and (iii) good faith.

As an illustration, let's assume that if *X* is *Y*, *A* can claim payment from *B*. Under that assumption, the first requirement of "appearance" shall be fulfilled, if *X* is not really *Y*, but, on the outside, it looks like so. The second requirement of "imputation" shall be met, if *B* is responsible for the creation of the appearance. And the third requirement of "good faith" shall be met, if *A* believes that the outward appearance fits the fact. So when all the three requirements are met, *A* can claim payment from *B*, as if *X* is truly *Y*. When the principle of the respect for outward appearance applies, *A* doesn't have to inquire into whether *X* is actually *Y*. Thus the principle promotes the safety of transactions, without slowing down their pace.

Back to our case, *A*'s expectation can be protected under Article 395 of the Commercial Act, which applies the principle of the respect for outward appearance to a transaction involving so called "apparent representative director" in Korean *pyon-hyon-dae-pyo-i-sa*. The article says, "A company shall be liable to a third party acting in good faith for any act done by a director who has used titles that can be understood as having authority to represent the company even where the said person has no such authority, such as president, vice president, executive director, or managing director."

Here the clause, "a third party acting in good faith" indicates the "good faith" requirement of the principle. And the clause, "any title such as president, vice-president, executive director, managing director, *etc.*" indicates the "appearance" requirement. And, even though te article is silent on the "imputation" requirement, it is generally understood that the principle applies only when a company allowed the use of such title as president *etc.*

In our case, *X* used a business card displaying her position as managing director. So the "appearance" requirement is met. And *A* believed that *X* is truly a representative director. So the "good faith" requirement is met. It's not clear whether the company *B* allowed *X* to use a title of representative director. So we can make only a qualified statement that if the company *B* allowed *X* to use the title, then the "imputation" requirement is also met. In conclusion, if all the three requirements are met, *A* can claim against *B* the fulfillment of the contract, as if *X* is truly a representative director.

C. Strict Liability

Back to our expressway analogy. Highways have intensive road signs to facilitate the safety of driving. However, those measures cannot be an absolute guarantee for safety. Accidents can happen despite all those measures for safety. And when they do, they tend to be big and nasty, as vehicle are moving so fast. Thus the drivers on highways have an obligation to watch the road conditions much more carefully than those on local roads. If an accident was caused by the carelessness of the driver, she bears a heavy burden of responsibility for the victims.

Likewise, commercial transactions carry much bigger risks than non-commercial transactions. When an accident happens, it can inflict huge losses on one of the parties. Thus the commercial law provides for two types of measures to address those risks. *First*, some provisions put heavier burden of responsibility on one of the parties. *Second*, other provisions impose collective liability upon the parties concerned. These provisions represent the "strict liability" feature of commercial law. Let's look at some examples of each type of measures.

1. Heavier Burden of Responsibility

We already studied one good example of the heavier burden of responsibility under the Commercial Act. You recall that, in a sale between only merchants, the buyer shall inspect the item purchased as soon as she receives it, and, if it has any defect, she has to notify it to the seller. In an ordinary sale under the Civil Act, the buyer has several months to inspect the item. But the Commercial Act puts heavier burden upon the buyer by demanding immediate inspection.

2. Collective Liaibility

Suppose that *A, B, C* and *D* are dining at a fine restaurant. *A* left the table first to wash her hands and did not return. *B* left the table to see what happed to *A* and did not return. And then *C* left the table to answer her cell phone and did not return. As the restaurant is closing up, *D* has to leave now. Here goes a question. Should *D* pay for all the foods, or only her own? The answer differs under the Civil Act and under the Commercial Act.

The Civil Act Article 408 says that, when more than one party are in debt, each debtor is proportionately liable, unless otherwise agreed. It means that, in principle, *D* needs only to pay for her own food. But if there is an agreement that the debtors are jointly liable, then *D* has to pay for all the food. The agreement here should exist between the debtors and the creditor, as well as between the debtors. In an ordinary situation, there is no express agreement on joint liability between a restaurant and its guests. But an agreement here can either be express or tacit.[21)] *A* tacit agreement can be presumed, if there are special circumstances, indicating that the resources of each debtor will jointly support the debt.[22)] So if there are such special circumstances, then *D* might have to pay for all the food. A good news for *D* is that the Supreme Court of Korea is quite reluctant to make such presumption of tacit agreement on joint liability.[23)] But a bad news is that *D* has to first persuade the manager to leave the restaurant. A litigation is costly, and the outcome is uncertain. At any rate, under the Civil Act, *D* needs only to pay for her own food in principle. In other words, proportional liability, or *boon-hal-chaeg-im* in Korean, between multiple debtors is a general rule under the Civil Act.

However, under the Commercial Act, joint liability, or *yon-dae-chaeg-im* in Korean, between multiple debtors shall be a general rule on certain conditions. Article 57(1) of the Act says, "If two or more persons assume obligations arising out of transactions that are commercial activities in respect of one or all of them, they shall be jointly and severally liable for the obligations." For example, if business partners borrowed some money for their business from other person, they shall be jointly liable for the debt, even without an agreement, express or tacit, on joint liability. Further, even if only one of the multiple debtors is a merchant, all the debtors shall still be jointly liable.

Let's look at an interesting Supreme Court decision on the issue.[24) Company *A* and its Representative Director *X* borrowed some money for a business project. Both *A* and *X* signed the IOU[25) as debtor. As we will see later, all the companies are merchant[26). But a representative director is just an organ of a company, *not* a merchant itself. So company *A* was a merchant, while *X* was not. However, as one of the debtors was a merchant, the Commercial Act Article 57 applied to the transaction, and both *A* and *X* were jointly liable for the debt.

Please also note here that Article 57(1) of the Act applies only to transactions where at least one of the debtors is a merchant. It doesn't matter whether any of the creditor is a merchant. If none of the debtors is a merchant, the provision does not apply, regardless of whether any of the creditors is a merchant.

CHAPTER Ⅱ
ORGANIZATIONAL FEATURES

Until now we have been studying various features of commercial law, and those features present themselves in the operation of businesses. So they are called the *operational* features of commercial law. Now let us turn to the *organizational* features of commercial law which present themselves in the organization of businesses. They include: easy supply of capital; easy supplement of labor; dispersion of risks; limitation of liability, and; preservation of businesses. Let's look at them one by one.

Ⅰ. EASY SUPPLY OF CAPITAL

Profit-making is a prime objective of business enterprises. The bigger they grow, the more profit they can make. Businesses need more money to grow bigger. The Civil Act provides for several measures to supply capital. But the Commercial Act provides for more efficient measures to facilitate the growth of businesses. Let us compare the measures availabel under the Civil Act, *i.e.*

partnership and loan, with the alternative measures available under the Commercial Act.

A. Partnership v. Measures under the Commercial Act

If a merchant does not have sufficient money for her business, she can invite a friend and form a partnership, in Korean *jo-hap*, under the Civil Act.[27)] But in general a partnership is suitable for small size businesses, as all the partners have to directly engage in major aspect of their businesses. So a big business needs more efficient measures for fund-raising that can minimize the interference in management. For example, the Commercial Act allows a corporation to issue shares, or *joo-sik* in Korean, to raise capital.[28)] As the price of each share is quite low, especially in comparison to the price of participation in a partnership, a corporation can raise a huge amount of money from the general public. As shareholders do not have to participate in the management of a corporation, the management may enjoy considerable discretion in its business activities, under the supervision of shareholders.

B. Loan v. Measures under the Commercial Act

A merchant can borrow some money from other person under the Civil Act provisions on loan for consumption.[29)] But business enterprises often need such a big amount of money that it cannot procure through a few individual arrangements of loan for consumption. Thus the Commercial Act provides for a measure for massive loan from the general public: a corporation may issue corporate bonds, or *sa-chae* in Korean, to the general public to raise funds.[30)] Just like shares, the price of each bond is quite low, and a corporation can raise a huge amount of money from the general public. Further, as bondholders are just creditors, not shareholders, they do not have the supervisory authority of shareholders. Thus the management of a corporation can raise a big fund by issuing bonds, without worrying about the interference by bondholders under normal circumstances.

Ⅱ. EASY SUPPLEMENT OF LABOR

By forming a partnership under the Civil Act, a merchant can also supplement labor. But she has to share discretion with her partners. Every major decisions shall require the consent of partners. If a merchant prefer an assistant who does not interfere with her own decision, she'd better hire an agent or employee under the Civil Act. But if a merchant wants to hire a number of agents and employees to build a highly structured business organization, she needs to be able to establish more sophisticated and diversified relationships with her in-house assistants. She also needs to enlist outside helpers fit to the purpose of her business.

Thus the Commercial Act provides for several measures for the supplement of labor which fit to the purpose of business organizations. *First*, an entrepreneur may establish a general partnership company or limited partnership company together with general partners who can contribute labor service to the company. *Second*, a merchant may hire commercial employees as in-house agents. *Third*, a merchant can enlist outside helpers, such as commercial agents, commercial brokers and commission agents. We will look into them in more details later[31].

Ⅲ. DISPERSION OF RISK

When a business enterprise grows big, thanks to the measures available under the Commercial Act, it gets to face huge risks that go way beyond what the small enterprises can imagine. A single entrepreneur cannot take the whole risk alone, and has to find a way to alleviate it. The Commercial Act provides for several measure for an entrepreneur to divide business risks with other parties. Let me give you a couple of examples.

A. Corporations

We already saw that a corporation can raise a huge amount of capital by issuing shares to the general public. As a result, big corporations used to have more than tens of thousands of shareholders. It means that its business risks are dispersed widely among those shareholders. Even if it goes broke, each shareholder shall bear only a very limited amount of loss. On the other hand, if a partnership goes broke, each partner shall bear significant losses, as there are only a few of them. Thus an entrepreneur can establish a corporation and issue its shares to the general public, and thereby disperse the huge business risks among numerous shareholders.

B. Insurances

I guess you are quite acquainted with how insurances, or *bo-hom* in Korean, work. For instance, if *A* has a house and worries about fire, she can buy a fire insurance. She pays a relatively small amount of money, called premium, or *bo-hom-ryo* in Korean, to the insurance company. When *A*'s house is on fire, the company pays *A* a big amount of money, called coverage or benefit, in Korean *bo-hom-gum*. As Article 638 of the Commercial Act says, "An insurance contract shall take effect when one of the parties pays the contractual premiums, and the other party promises to pay a certain amount of insurance coverage or other benefits upon occurrence of an uncertain event against the property, life, or body of the former." Among the numerous buyers of fire insurance, only a few suffer from a fire. As a result, each buyer has only to pay a small amount of money to raise a fund big enough to cover the damage from the fire. Thus insurance is another measure for the dispersion of risk among numerous parties, available under the Commercial Act.

Ⅳ. LIMITATION OF LIABILITY

When a person borrows some money from other person, she is supposed to repay the whole amount of money. Sometimes, of course, she also has to pay the interest. It might be unthinkable for an honest person to repay only a part of the money that she borrowed. We can say that debtors in general bear *unlimited* liability for their debts. In other words, a debtor shall pay the last dime of her debt. But the Commercial Act grants a privilege of *limited* liability to a certain members of companies. There are five types of companies under the Commercial Act. Some of them has partners with unlimited liability. We call them general partners, or *moo-han-chage-im-sa-won* in Korean. But others have partners or investors with limited liability. We call them limited partners, or *yoo-han-chaeg-im-sa-won* in Korean. The composition of partners in each company under the Commercial Act is as follows:

- A general partnership company, or *hap-myong-hoe-sa* in Korean, has more than two general partners.
- A limited partnership company, or *hap-ja-hoe-sa* in Korean, has more than one general partner and more than one limited partner.
- A corporation, or *joo-sik-hoe-sa* in Korean, has more than one limited partner, called shareholder, in Korean *joo-joo*.
- A limited company, or *yoo-han-hoe-sa* in Korean, has more than one limited partner.
- A limited liability company, or *yoo-han-chaeg-im-hoe-sa* in Korean, has more than one limited partner.

General partners have to pay the last dime of their companies' debt. But limited partners do not have to repay the whole debt. At worst they lose only their investment in the companies, and no more. When a creditor fails to get her money back out of a company's assets, she can seize a property of unlimited partners. But, as a general rule, she may not go for the property of limited partners.

Why does the Commercial Act grant such an exceptional privilege to the limited partners of a company? It's because the Act wants to promote investment and facilitate entrepreneurship by limiting the liability of investors. Thanks to the limitation of liability, general partners of a limited partnership company can invite investors as limited partners to their risky businesses. Further, companies with only limited partners, such as corporations, limited companies and limited liability companies, could go for hazardous enterprises, leading technological innovations and developing new markets. Especially, corporations can undertake ventures in the largest scale, as they can invite numerous shareholders who has only to invest a small amount of money, enjoying the privilege of limited liability. Thus, among other things, the limitation of liability has significantly contributed to the development of technology and the growth of economy, by encouraging businesses to go for risky enterprises.

V. PRESERVATION OF BUSINESS

The Commercial Act promotes the maintenance and preservation of businesses with a variety of measures. Let me take a few examples.

First, the Act separates a corporation from its shareholders. As a corporation is an independent legal entity, separate from its investors, *i.e.* shareholders, it can continue to exist despite the changes in the ownership of shares.

Second, the Act demands the capital adequacy, or *ja-bon-gum-choong-sil* of a corporation to preserve sufficient assets for the company itself and its creditors. As we just saw, a corporation has limited partners only. Its creditors can get their money back only from the company's assets. Thus the Act contains several strict regulations on a corporation's capital, reserve funds and accounting in order to preserve sufficient assets for its creditors.

Third, the Act allows the maintenance of agency authority in case of a principal's decease. Under the Civil Act Article 127(i) an agency authority shall be extinguished when the principal dies. But the Commercial Act Article 50 says, "Agency rights granted by a merchant in respect of his or her business shall not be extinguished by reason of death of the principal." The Commercial Act provides for an exception for the Civil Act principle, in order to preserve businesses even in case of a principal merchant's death.

CHAPTER Ⅲ INCLINATION OF COMMERCIAL LAW

We just have surveyed the operational and the organizational features of commercial law. If commercial law is a car, these features are the attributes of the car itself. Now let us see which direction the commercial law car is going. Commercial law is said to have two distinct inclination: progressiveness and inclination toward global coordination.

Ⅰ. PROGRESSIVENESS

Commercial law tends to be more flexible and progressive than civil law, as the former has to adapt to the rapidly changing economic environment and constantly emerging new business models. In a relative sense, civil law has more conservative and traditional tendency than the commercial law.

Ⅱ. INCLINATION TOWARD GLOBAL COORDINATION

Commercial law pursues economic rationality, a quite universal goal for merchants across the globe. It also reflects the globalization of business activities. Thus commercial law tends towards global coordination. Especially in the areas where vigorous international exchanges are taking place, such as international trade, marine transport, checks and promissory notes, numerous international treaties have been concluded. United Nations Convention on Contracts for the International Sale of Goods (CISG) is just one of the remarkable examples.

Now we finished looking at all the special features of commercial law. The long preview has ended, and, in the next part, we will start watching the feature presentation of commercial law drama.

PART III

GENERAL PROVISIONS

CHAPTER I MERCHANTS

I. WHO IS A MERCHANT?

The feature presentation of commercial law drama starts with the inquiry into the leading role: the merchant, or *sang-in* in Korean. A merchant is a legal entity who operates a business. The Commercial Act applies to a certain range of transactions which a merchant engages in. To be more precise, the Commercial Act applies to commercial activities, in Korean *sang-haeng-wi*, and, commercial activities are certain kinds of transactions in which, at least, a merchant participates as a party.

There are two types of commercial activities: unilateral commercial activities, or *il-bang-jok sang-haeng-wi* in Korean, and reciprocal commercial activities, or *ssang-bang-jok sang-haeng-wi* in Korean. The former is a transaction in which only one of the parties is a merchant, *e.g.* a sale between a retailer and a consumer. The latter is a transaction where both of the parties are merchants, *e.g.* a sale between a retailer and a wholesaler. Most provisions of the Commercial Act apply to both unilateral and reciprocal commercial activities. But some harsh provisions apply only to reciprocal commercial activities. For instance, the provisions on sales in Part 2 Chapter 2 of the Commercial Act apply only to sales between merchants. We already looked at one of those provisions, concerning buyer's duty of immediate inspection.

Anyway the concept of a merchant is a cornerstone of the Commercial Act, as it forms the basis to determine the coverage of the Act. However, it is practically impossible to define a merchant solely on the ground of the substance of her business, as there exist such a numerous types of businesses, and new business models are constantly emerging. Thus the Commercial Act prescribes two main categories of merchants: merchants-by nature of business, in Korean *dang-yon-sang-in*, and merchants-by legal construction, in Korean *ui-je-sang-in*. *First*, merchants-by nature of business are those who engage in one of the well-established types of businesses listed in Article 46 of the Act. The concept is based on the substance or the nature of a merchant's business. That's why we call them merchants-by nature of business. *Second*, merchants-by legal construction are those who engage in a type of business which is not listed in Article 46 of the Act, but run their businesses with a merchant's equipment and method. The concept is based on the form or style of a merchant's business rather than its substance or nature. Thus it can embrace all the variety of business models that are not yet covered by Article 46. Merchants-by legal construction are divided again into two subgroups: merchants-by equipment, in Korean *sol-*

bi-sang-in, and civil companies, in Korean *min-sa-hoe-sa*.

Besides the Commercial Act Article 9 says that small-size businesses, called petty merchants, in Korean *so-sang-in*, shall be immune from some of its burdensome provisions. They are contrasted with common merchants which include both merchants-by nature of business and merchants-by legal construction.

Here is a summary of the classification of merchants under the Commercial Act.

- Common merchants
  - Merchants-by nature of business
  - Merchants-by legal construction
    - Merchants-by equipment
    - Civil companies
- Petty merchants

Now let's look into each type of merchants in some more details.

Ⅱ. MERCHANTS-BY NATURE OF BUSINESS

A merchant-by nature of business is a person who engages in basic commercial activities listed in Article 46 of the Commercial Act, in her own name.

"In her own *name*" here means that all the rights and duties stemming from the activities belong to her. On the other hand, when a person concludes a contract "on her *account*", all the benefits and losses incurred by the transaction belong to her. In other words, the phrase "in her own name" relates to the legal consequences of a transaction, while the phrase "on her account" refers to its economic consequences. Thus if *A* is a financier of a business who takes all the profit and loss, but *B* runs the business in her own name, then *B* is the merchant, not *A*.

As I told you earlier the Commercial Act Article 46 lists well-established types of businesses[32]. It's quite a long list containing 22 subparagraphs. Let's just briefly look over the list, without delving into each subparagraph.

At the top, we can find the two most time-honored business types: sales in subparagraph 1 and lease in subparagraph 2. They are followed by the secondary industry: manufacturing, processing and repairing in subparagraph 3. Then subparagraph 4 refers to public utility business, and subparagraph 5 contracting business, in Korean *do-gup*. The next two subparagraphs lists relatively modern industries: publishing, printing and photographing in subparagraph 6 and advertisements, communications and information in subparagraph 7. And subparagraph 8 refers to financial business.

The next six subparagraphs, from subparagraph 9 to 14, refer to another familiar group of businesses: hospitality business; businesses of commercial agents, commercial brokers and commission agents; transportation business and warehousing business. The Commercial Act contains separate chapters for each type of those businesses, from Chapter 5 to 11 of Part 2 of the Act. Later we will investigate into each of them more closely[33].

Next, subparagraph 15 refers to trust business, and subparagraph 16 mutual savings account business. "Mutual savings account," or *sang-ho-boo-gum* in Korean, here means a unique financial system in Korea through which low-incomers and small businesses can help each other for petty loans. Then subparagraph 17 refers to insurance. The Commercial Act has a separate part, *i.e.* Part 4, for insurance alone. And subparagraph 18 refers to mining industry which belongs to the primary industry.

The last 4 subparagraphs were introduced quite recently; subparagraphs 19, 20 and 21 in 1995 and subparagraph 22 in 2010. They cover the newly developed business models which have enjoyed such a rapid growth that it was imperative to put them on the list of commercial activities. They are: financial lease in subparagraph 19, franchise in subparagraph 20, factoring in subparagraph 21, and payment settlement business in subparagraph 22. The Commercial Act has separate chapters for the first three of them, Chapters 12, 13 and 14 of Part 2 of the Act.

To sum up, most of the business types listed in Article 46 of the

Commercial Act belong to the tertiary industry. The list also includes the secondary industry, *i.e.* manufacturing, processing and repairing in subparagraph 3. Among the first industry it includes only mining industry in subparagraph 18. Agriculture, stockbreeding and fishery are not on the list.

One more note: even if a person engages in one of the basic commercial activities listed in Article 46, she should fulfill an additional requirement to be a merchant-by nature of business. She should do that “as business”. In other words, she should repeatedly and continuously engage in the same type of activities on profit making purpose. If she engages in a one-time transaction or if she does it without any profit-making purpose, the activity is not a basic commercial activity, and consequently she is not a merchant-by nature of business. Further, according to the proviso of the article, if a person manufactures goods or renders services solely for the purpose of earning wages, her activity is not a basic commercial activity, and therefore she is not a merchant-by nature of business. Porters and needle workers are the examples. As their businesses are so small, it is not appropriate to apply the Commercial Act to their activities.[34)]

Ⅲ. MERCHANTS-BY LEGAL CONSTRUCTION

As we already saw merchants-by legal construction do not engage in any one of the business types listed in Article 46 of the Commercial Act. But they are deemed to be a merchant on the basis of the form or style of their businesses. There are two types of merchants-by legal construction: merchants-by equipment and civil companies.

A. Merchants-By Equipment

Article 5(1) of the Commercial Act prescribes the definition of a merchant-by equipment as follows: "Any person who engages in any business in the same manner as a merchant through a store or similar facility shall be deemed a merchant, even if he or she does not carry out commercial activities." "Commercial activities" here indicates the basic commercial activities listed in Article 46. "In a merchant's way" means that the person is using measures generally accepted as a merchant's business methods, such as stores, offices, trade names, trade (accounting) books and commercial employees.

The concept of merchants-by equipment enables the Commercial Act to apply to business types that are not covered by Article 46. It can be an old type of business, such as agriculture, stockbreeding and fishery. Or it can be a whole new business model that has emerged just recently. For example, a farmer is not a merchant-by nature of business. But if a farmer sells her product in a merchant's way maintaining a shop or similar equipment, she can be a merchant-by legal construction. The Supreme Court of Korea said that a person who runs a private academy, in Korean *hag-won*, can be a merchant-by legal construction.[35] But the Court opined that a lawyer cannot be a merchant-by legal construction, due to the public nature of her job.[36]

B. Civil Companies

Under the Commercial Act all the companies are merchants. If a company engages in one of the basic commercial activities listed in Article 46, it is a merchant-by nature of business (Article 4). If it engages in a business which is not covered by Article 46, it still is a merchant-by legal construction (Article 5(2)). The former is called a commercial company, and the latter a civil company. As a company is the most sophisticated form of business organization, a company represents the core of merchants' method or style. Thus the Commercial Act treats civil companies in exactly the same way as commercial companies.

Ⅳ. PETTY MERCHANTS

We saw that the Commercial Act exempts petty merchants from its burdensome provisions, due to its small size. Article 2 of the Enforcement Decree, in Korean *si-haeng-ryong*, of the Act prescribes the two requirements to be a petty merchant. *First*, her equity capital does not amount to KRW 10 million. "Equity capital" here means the present price of her overall business assets. As KRW 10million is such a small amount, even some merchants with a food cart might not qualify for a petty merchant. Street vendors or peddlers might be an apt example of petty merchants. *Second*, she shall not be a company. As a company is the most sophisticated form of business organization, it shall not be exempt from any provisions of the Commercial Act, even if its equity capital does not amount to KRW 10 million. The Act exempts petty merchants from the provisions concerning managers, trade names, commercial books and commercial registration.

With this we finished looking at all the types of merchants under the Commercial Act. In the next chapter we will investigate one of the supporting roles in the commercial law drama: a commercial employee.

CHAPTER Ⅱ COMMERCIAL EMPLOYEES

Ⅰ. HELPERS OF A MERCHANT

A merchant can enlist three types of aides or helpers under the Commercial Act. *First*, commercial employees, in Korean *sang-op-sa-yong-in*, as in-house agents. *Second*, external helpers such as commercial agents, commercial brokers, commission agents, carriers, transportation brokers, and warehousemen. *Third*, organs, in Korean *gi-gwan*, of a company.

The last one warrants some more explanation. As we saw earlier, a company and its partners, or investors, are separate legal entities[37]. A company may have its own rights and duties. For example, a company can acquire the ownership of its own office building. In that case the partners does not have any direct ownership of the property. They just have their stakes in the company. But how can a company acquire the ownership of a property? It doesn't have eyes to read documents, nor a brain to make decisions, nor a hand to sign contracts. How could a company make deals without a body? The answer is that it needs help from natural persons who have flesh and bones. That is, a company shall appoint natural persons as organs. “Organs” here is a quite metaphoric expression which means that those natural persons shall be the eyes, brains and hands of a company. For example, a corporation shall appoint Representative Dirctors or Chief Executive Officers (CEOs), and grant them representative authority to conduct its transactions. When a Representative Director or a CEO sings a contract on behalf of a company, the company shall be bound by the contract.

Back to the aides of a merchant. As we will look into external helpers later in detail[38], our focus here shall be placed on the in-house agents, *i.e.* commercial employees.

Ⅱ. WHO IS A COMMERCIAL EMPLOYEE?

A commercial employee is an agent of a specific merchant, who assists the merchant at all times in his external business under the command of the merchant. Let’s divide the concept into two parts and look at them one by one.

First, a commercial employee belongs to a specified merchant. “Belong” here means that she is an in-house aide and gets instructions from the merchant. On the other hand, directors, in Korean *i-sa*, and managing general partners, in Korean *op-moo-jip-haeng-sa-won*, are organs of a company, not in-house aides. But the

Supreme Court said that, if a director holds an additional position as commercial employee, the Commercial Act provisions on commercial employees shall also apply.[39] Outside helpers, such as commercial agents, are independent merchants themselves, and do not belong to other merchants. So they are distinguished from commercial employees.

Second, a commercial employee shall have agency authority or agency power, in Korean *dae-ri-gwon*, to assist the principal merchant in her external business with clients. Employees without agency authority, such as cashiers and reporters, are not commercial employees. Despite the title, commercial employee, employment relationship with the merchant is not required, as long as she has agency authority. For example, a family member can be a commercial employee of a merchant without any employment contract.

Ⅲ. TYPES OF COMMERCIAL EMPLOYEES

The Commercial Act classifies commercial employees into three categories by the scope of their agency power: managers, department leaders and shop assistants. *First*, managers, in Korean *ji-bae-in*, who have truly comprehensive agency power. *Second*, department leaders, such as section chiefs, in Korean *gwa-jang*, and deputies, in Korean *dae-ri*, who have partially comprehensive agency power. “Partially” and “comprehensive” here contradict each other. In other words it is an oxymoron. We will explore the reason for the terminology later[40]. *Third*, shop assistants, in Korean *jom-won*. Let’s look into each type of commercial employees.

A. Managers

According to the Commercial Act Article 11, a manager is a commercial employee who “may perform all judicial and extrajudicial acts on behalf of the business proprietor, relating to her business.” As a manager has truly comprehensive agency power, called Prokura, in Korean *ji-bae-gwon*, relating to the principal merchant’s business, her clients do not have to investigate the scope of her authority. Thus the comprehensive agency power of a manager substantially contribute to the safety of trade.

A manager can do virtually anything, concerning a merchant’s business. She can not only conclude a contract on behalf of a merchant, which is an extrajudicial act, but also represent the merchant in a court room, which is a judicial act. The latter part is an important exception to the rule that only attorneys-at-law may conduct judicial acts under Article 87 of the Civil Procedure Act, in Korean *min-sa-so-song-bop*. But there are a couple of things that a manager may not do, even within the scope of a merchant’s business. *First*, a manager may not appoint or dismiss another manager. As a manger is an *alter ego* of the principal merchant, only the merchant herself may create one. Even a manger may not hire another manager, unless the merchant grants special authority to do that (Commercial Act Article 11(2)). *Second*, she may not abolish or transfer the business, as the agency power of a manager presupposes the existence of a business of her boss.

B. Apparent Managers

Here let's consider a case where an employee of a merchant uses a typical title of a manager, but is not actually a manager.

> **[CASE]** Sharon is not a manager. But she has used business cards representing herself as "Head of Business" employed by a manufacturer. She ordered steel pipes on behalf of her employer. But her employer refuses to pay for them on the ground that she lacks the agency authority of a manager. Could the supplier claim for the execution of the contract against the manufacturer?

The Commercial Act Article 11 calls a commercial employee with a truly comprehensive agency authority a "manager." But in practice managers have a variety of titles, such as the head of business of a branch office, in Korean *ji-jom-jang*, and the director of the headquarters, in Korean *bon-boo-jang*, as Article 14 of the

Commercial Act illustrates. Chief of local office, in Korean *chool-jang-so-jang*, and head of business office, in Korean *yong-op-so-jang*, are another examples.

When you deal with a person using such a title, you expect that she is a manager who can do anything concerning the business of her boss. It hardly comes to your mind that you might have to check the commercial registry to see if she is really a manager. So you proceed to negotiate with her for a deal. Later if it turns out that she is not actually a manager, and the deal that you negotiated with her is void, it will be a disaster for you. If the law allows for such an outrageous consequence, the safety of trade shall be seriously hampered: you should investigate into the competence of your counterpart whenever you make a deal.

Thus the main sentence of Article 14(1) of the Commercial Act says, "A person with a title of head of the principal office or a branch office, or any other person with a title recognized as equivalent to a manager shall be deemed to have the same authority as a manager at the principal office or a branch office." It means that if an employee uses a typical title of a manager, she is deemed to have the same authority as a manager, even if she is not actually one. The article calls such an employee an "apparent manager," in Korean *pyo-hyon-ji-bae-in*. If you make a deal with an apparent manager, the deal is valid and her boss has to fulfill the contract.

But there are some preconditions that have to be met.

It is generally understood that the article is based on the principle of respect for outward appearance that we already studied. Thus the article shall apply to a transaction only when the three elements or requirements of the principle are met: appearance, imputation and good faith. *First*, "appearance" requirement is met, if an employee uses one of the typical titles of a manager. *Second*, "imputation" requirement is met, if her boss permits the use of such a title. The permission doesn't have to be express. A tacit permission also can fulfill the requirement. *Third*, "good faith" requirement is met, if the other party believes that she actually has adequate agency power. So the Commercial Act Article 14(2) says, "The provisions of paragraph (1) shall not apply where the other party has acted in bad faith."

When all the above three requirements are met, the employee shall be regarded as an apparent manger. It doesn't mean that she shall be promoted to a manager. It's just that she shall be deemed to have adequate agency power of a manager regarding a particular transaction, and that the deal she made shall bind her boss. Please also note that, according to the proviso of the Commercial Act Article 14, it applies only to extrajudicial acts.

Back to our case of Sharon. It is obvious that the first requirement of "appearance" is fulfilled. She used a typical title of a manager, *i.e.* Head of Business, on her business card. But it is not clear whether the other two requirements are met. So we can only make a conditional statement here: (i) if Sharon's boss gave a permission, express or tacit, to use such a title, *and* (ii) if the supplier did not know that Sharon lacked adequate agency authority of a manager, then the supplier may claim the execution of the contract against the manufacturer.

C. Department Leaders

When a merchant has several employees, she might organize them into a few groups, called departments or sections. A typical hierarchy of Korean business organization is as follows: at the top it has departments, in Korean *boo*; departments have sections, in Korean *gwa*; sections have subsections, in Korean *gye*. Recently more and more business organizations have teams at the same level as departments or sections. As it will be very inefficient for the merchant to engage in all the deals that each group makes, she grants the chief or deputy of each group a quite comprehensive agency authority within the range of each group's business. For example, the head of sales department can do anything concerning sales, and the chief of materials section can do anything concerning supply of materials. Deputies, such as deputy head of department, in Korean *cha-jang*, and deputy section chief, in Korean *dae-ri*, also have a comprehensive agency power concerning the business of their departments or sections.

Article 15 of the Commercial Act prescribes the competence of those section chiefs and deputies, calling them "employee invested with partial comprehensive agency authority." It's quite a long title. So, let us simply call them "department leaders," for your convenience. It's not exactly a legal term, but quite clearly describe their roles and competence in a business organization. They are kind of "managers in their own departments," capable of doing anything within departmental limits. But, please, beware that there's an important difference between a department leader and a real manager: the former may not represent her principal merchant at the court of law. As Article 15(1) says, "An employee who has been entrusted with certain branches of business or specified matters relating to business may effect all acts other than judicial acts."

D. Shop Assistants

Suppose that you visited a shop looking for an item. A person working at the shop approached you to recommend a few brands. You picked one of them and negotiated the price with her. She gave you a surprisingly generous discount. You left the shop with a happy smile. But your cell phone rang when you arrived home. It was the shop owner. She said that the person that you negotiated with was just an apprentice and had no authority to sell goods, not to mention an authority to give discounts. She contended that the deal was void and you had to return the stuff. What do you think of her claim?

If the deal was void on the ground that the person working at a shop actually does not have any authority to sell goods, a customer shall have to check the competence of a person working at the shop, before she buys a stuff. But I'm sure you never have asked a person working at a shop whether she has appropriate agency authority. Such an inquiry is simply impractical. A shop assistant is supposed to have adequate agency authority to sell goods. If she doesn't have any such authority, she should have told the truth to the customer in the first place to avoid meaningless negotiation. In other words, a customer usually expects that a shop assistant has an agency authority to sell goods, and such an expectation has to be fulfilled. If the law denies the expectation, it will seriously hinder the safety of transaction.

Thus Article 16(1) of the Commercial Act says, "An employee of a store selling goods shall be deemed to have all the authority in regard to the sale of goods at that store." "All the authority" here includes the power concerning discounts, exchange, sales on credit, *etc.*[41)]

It is generally understood that the article is based on the principle of respect for outward appearance. I assume that you recall the three elements or requirements of the principle: appearance, imputation and good faith. *First*, "appearance" requirement is fulfilled by the very fact that the assistant works at a shop selling goods. *Second*, "imputation" requirement is fulfilled if the shop owner permitted the assistant to work at the shop. The permission shall either be express or tacit. *Third*, "good faith" requirement is fulfilled if the customer believed that the assistant had adequate agency power. Article 16 does not directly refer to the third requirement of good faith. Instead Article 16(2) says that Article 14(2), which prescribes the good-faith requirement, shall apply *mutatis mutandis*, that is, with some necessary changes.[42)]

Although the Commercial Act Article 16 refers only to an employee of a shop selling goods, the general opinion says that the coverage of the article could be extended to an employee of a hospitality business operator, such as theaters, hotels and restaurants.[43)] Suppose that you went to a vacation to a faraway place. You found a motel with a signboard, saying that the room charge is KRW 100,000 per night. You skillfully negotiated with a clerk and received a 50% discount. After you left the motel next morning, you got a phone call. It was the motel owner, saying that the clerk you negotiated with was just an apprentice without any agency authority. A different place, but the same issue. As long as the three requirements for the respect of outward appearance are met, the deal shall remain valid, even if the clerk actually had no agency authority.

Ⅳ. DUTY OF COMMERCIAL EMPLOYEES

[CASE] Michel is the owner of a restaurant serving traditional Korean food. Her manager launched his own restaurant in a neighboring town, serving Thai food. Is there any remedy available for Michel to get compensated for her loss incurred by her manager's Thai food business?

A. Issues

The case concerns the duty of commercial employee to prohibit competitive business, in Korean *gyong-op-pi-ji-ui-mu*, under Article 17 of the Commercial Act. Unlike its name, it actually has two parts: *first*, the duty to prohibit business in competition with her employer, and; *second*, the duty to prohibit two-jobs. The former, non-compete obligation, keeps a commercial employee from in-juring the business interest of her employer by exploiting inside information. The latter, dual office ban, prevents a commercial employee from being distracted from her employer's business.

B. Non-Compete Obligation

In order to find a breach on non-compete obligation, three

requirements have to be met. *First*, a commercial employee conducts any transaction falling in the same class of business as that of her employer. The transaction does not have to be the exactly same type as that of the employer. It needs only to be in competition with that of the employer. For instance, a commercial employee of a soft drink manufacturer may not engage in ice cream business, if soft drinks and ice cream are, at least partially, in competition with each other. *Second*, the transaction is conducted on the employee's account or on the account of a person other than the employer. It means that the profit from the transaction does not go to the employer, but to somebody else. *Third*, the transaction is conducted without the permission by the employer.

If a commercial employee conducted any such transaction without the employer's approval, she can fire the employee and/or claim damages against her. However, damage claims might get quite tricky, as it is often very hard to prove damages. Suppose that *X* is a manager of *Y*'s café. *X* opens her own café in April. *X* and *Y* are in direct competition with each other in their businesses. In March, before *X* opens the café, *Y*'s revenue was KRW 5 million. In April, *X* earned the revenue of KRW 2 million, while *Y*'s revenue was KRW 4 million. How much loss did *Y* suffer due to the café business of *X*? Does all the revenue that *X* earned in April, which is KRW 2 million, has to be regarded as the loss of *Y*? Or only the decrease in *Y*'s revenue in April, which is KRW 1 million, has to be regarded as *Y*'s loss? Maybe the answer is neither. The loss could be more than KRW 2 million, if *Y*'s average revenue in April was KRW 7 million, and she suffered KRW 3 million decrease in April's revenue. On the contrary, the loss could be less than KRW 1 million, if a part of the decrease in *Y*'s revenue was caused by other factors, such as recession. The estimation of *Y*'s loss can be trickier, if *Y*'s revenue increased in April, say to KRW 6 million. In any case, *Y* has to prove her loss to claim damage against *X*. The burden of proof shall be placed on *Y*, not *X*. If *Y* fails to prove the amount of her damage, she might not get any compensation.

Thus the Commercial Act provides additional remedy for the employer that doesn't require any proof of damage. The remedy works in two ways.

First, if a commercial employee conducts such transaction on her account, the employer may regard the transaction as conducted on the employer's own account. Then all the economic consequences (*i.e.* profit and loss) of the transaction belong to the employer. For example, if a commercial employee concludes a supply contract with a third party, her employer may regard the transaction as conducted on the employer's account so that the employer can get all the profits. Of course, the employer shall pay all the cost, too, as all the economic consequences shall belong to the employer. But, please, note that all the legal consequences still belong to the commercial employee. If the commercial employee supplied a product with defect to the third party, the employee shall be responsible for the defect, not the employer.

Second, if a commercial employee conducted such transaction on other person's account, the employer can require the employee to transfer the benefit she got from the transaction. Suppose that a commercial employee *A* conducted a transaction in competition with her employer *B*. The transaction was conducted on the account of *A*'s friend *C*. In that case, *B* may not regard the transaction as conducted on her own account. But she may require *A* to transfer the benefit, such as commission, that *A* received from *C*.

In both cases the employer can deprive the commercial employee of the benefit that she gained from the breach of her duty not to compete with her own boss. The Commercial Act calls this special right of employer "intervention right," or *gae-ip-gwon* in Korean.

C. Dual office ban

A commercial employee shall become neither an unlimited partner, nor a director of a company. He also shall not become an employee of other merchant. The majority of commentators say that the company or the other merchant, who hires the employee, need not be in competition with the employer.[44] If a commercial employee breached the dual office ban, the employer may fire the employee and/or claim damages against her. But the Commercial Act does not grant intervention right to the employer in that situation.

D. Conclusion

Back to our case. As Michel's manager opened his own restaurant, the dual office ban is not the issue here. So let's consider whether the three requirements for the breach of non-compete obligation were met. *First*, as the manager opened his own restaurant, it is evident that the transactions at the restaurant was not conducted on Michel's account. But it's not clear whether they were conducted on the manager's account. *Second*, it might be controversial whether a traditional Korean food restaurant and a Thai food restaurant are in competition with each other. If they are in competition at least partly, the transactions at both restaurants fall in the same class of transaction. *Third*, it is not obvious whether Michel gave permission to the manager to open the restaurant. So we can make a conditional statement here that, if Michel did not give permission to the manager, the latter breaches the non-compete obligation of a commercial employee.

About the remedy. Michel can claim damage against the manager, if she can prove it. But, even if she cannot do that, she still can exert the intervention right under Article 17 of the Commercial Act. If the transactions were conducted on the manager's account, Michel may regard them as conducted on her own account. If they were conducted on a third party's account, she may request the manager to transfer the benefit from the transactions.

CHAPTER Ⅲ TRADE NAMES

Ⅰ. CONCEPT OF TRADE NAME

A trade name, or *sang-ho* in Korean, is a title that a merchant uses to represent herself in her business. A title of non-merchant is not a trade name. For example, a lawyer's title may not be registered as a trade name.[45] Full names and stage names that are used in a nonbusiness context are not trade names. A trade name is written in letters, unlike a trade mark which is displayed in shapes.

Ⅱ. CHOICE OF TRADE NAME

The Commercial Act Article 18 adopts the principle of free choice of trade name, and says that a merchant may choose her name or other titles as her trade name. Thus a trade name needs not reflect the true substance of a merchant's business. For instance, "New York Bakery" can be used by a merchant who neither has been in New York, nor uses any New York style recipe.

However, there are a few exceptions for the principle under the

Commercial Act. *First*, the lettering "partnership company," "limited partnership company," "limited liability company," "stock company" or "limited company" shall be contained in the trade name of a company according to its nature (Article 19). *Second*, no person, other than a company, may use in the trade name any lettering indicating a company. This shall also apply where a person has acquired the business of a company (Article 20). *Third*, no person shall, for any unfair purpose, use any trade name likely to induce others to believe that it represents the business of other person (Article 23(1)).

Ⅲ. RIGHT TO A TRADE NAME

A merchant's right to a trade name consists of two parts: (i) the right to use the trade name in signboards and business documents, *etc.*; and (ii) the right to exclusivity which prohibits others from using trade names causing misconception on the ownership of business.

General opinion says that a right to a trade name has both the attributes of a property right and those of a right to personality. Thus it has economic value and can be transferred, while Its infringement may cause damage to the merchant's credibility.

A. Right to Exclusivity of Trade Name

1. Remedies Against Infringement

Now let's look more closely at the right to exclusivity of trade name. Under the Commercial Act three types of remedies are available against a breach of the right to exclusivity of trade name: (i) claim for abolition of similar trade names; (ii) claim for damages; and (iii) administrative fines. Let us investigate them one by one.

2. Claim for Abolition of Similar Trade Names

According to the Commercial Act Article 23(1) and (2), the prerequisites for the claim for abolition of similar trade names are threefold. *First*, the trade name is likely to induce others to believe that it represents the business of another person. For example, if a big company leasing telecommunication facilities uses a trade name similar to that of a small company selling electronic goods, it's not an infringement.[46)] *Second*, the violator uses the trade name for unfair purpose. For instance, if a person used a signboard displaying the trade name "New Seoul Photo Studio" together with a subtitle, "former Hoba-Hoba Photo Studio," he is regarded to have used it for an unfair purpose.[47)] *Third*, the interest of the claimant is likely to be harmed.

When all these prerequisites are met, the right holder may claim for (i) the prohibition of current and future use of the trade name, and (ii) the cancellation of the registration. Even if the trade name of claimant has not been registered, she may still claim for the cancellation.

3. Claim for Damages

If the unfair use of trade name caused damages to the claimant (*e.g.* damages to her credibility), she can claim damages against the violator, together with the abolition of trade name (Commercial Act Article 23(3)).

4. Administrative Fines

A fine under KRW 2 million can be levied on the infringement of the right to exclusivity of trade name (Commercial Act Article 28).

B. Reinforcing Right to Exclusivity by Registration

We saw that the Commercial Act strongly supports a right to exclusivity of trade name. But a merchant can reinforce his right to exclusivity of a trade name by registering it on the commercial registry. That is, the registration of trade name (i) relaxes the prerequisites for claim for abolition of similar trade names, and (ii) prohibits the registration of the same trade name.

1. Relaxing the Prerequisites for Claim for Abolition of Similar Trade Names

If a merchant registers her trade name on the commercial registry, she can claim the abolition of similar trade names more easily. *First*, any person who uses the registered trade name of another person in the same Special Metropolitan City, Metropolitan City, and Si/Gun, in respect of the same type of business shall be presumed to have done so for an unfair purpose (Commercial Act Article 23(4)). The burden of proof is shifted to the claimee. *Second*, the claimant needs not prove that she is likely to be harmed.[48)]

2. Prohibiting the Registration of the Same Trade Name

No trade name registered by another person shall be registered as a trade name of the same kind of business in the same Special Metropolitan City, Metropolitan City, or Si/Gun (Commercial Act Article 22). A merchant may claim the exclusion of registration, only when another person tries to register exactly the same trade name as her own.

If another person somehow registered exactly the same trade

name as her own, a merchant may claim the cancellation of registration under the Commercial Act Article 22.[49] However, if the trade name registered earlier is not exactly the same as that registered later, the registration of the latter shall not be cancelled.[50]

Ⅳ. LIABILITY OF A NAME LENDER

A. Concept

The Commercial Act Article 24 talks about the liability of persons who have lent their names. It says, "Any person who has permitted another person to carry on business using his or her name or trade name shall be liable jointly and severally with the person borrowing his or her name in respect of any obligations arising from a transaction in favor of a third party who has effected such transaction in the belief that such person borrowing the name is the business owner." The liability of a name lender, in Korean *myong-ui-dae-yo-ja-ui chaeg-im*, under the article facilitates the safety of trade by protecting a third party who trusted outward appearance. That is, as you might already noticed, the article is based on the principle of respect for outward appearance which we surveyed earlier[51].

B. Prerequisites

I assume you recall the three prerequisites of the principle of respect for outward appearance: (i) outward appearance, (ii) imputation and (iii) good faith. Reading the Commercial Act Article 24, you could easily figure out how the three requirements can be fulfilled in the context of the liability of name lender: (i) the "outward-appearance" requirement can be met when a person (hereinafter "borrower") carries on business using the title of other person (hereinafter "name lender"); (ii) the "imputation" requirement can be satisfied when a name lender permitted a borrower to use his title; and (iii) the "good-faith" requirement can be accommodated when a third party trusts in the outward appearance described above. However, let us go a little deeper into some interesting issues, concerning those three requirements.

1. Outward Appearance

a. Use of "Name or Trade Name"

The name or trade name that a borrower uses does not have to be identical to that of a name lender. It is sufficient that a borrower uses similar name or trade name that could be recognized as name lender's title. For example, if the lender's trade name is *X*, "the Branch Office of *X*" may fulfill the "outward appearance" requirement.[52] However, "the Commercial Agent of *X*" may *not* fulfill the requirement, as a commercial agent is an independent merchant himself.[53)]

A name lender does not have to be a merchant. For instance, Incheon Metropolitan City can be a name lender.[54)]

b. "Use" of Name or Trade Name

If *X* let *Y* use his shop, telephone and warehouse, but *Y* did not use *X*'s name or trade name, it may not fulfill the outward-appearance requirement.[55)]

c. "Business Operation" Using Name or Trade Name

Even if a name lender and a borrower engage in different types of businesses, the outward-appearance requirement could still be fulfilled. For example, if a hotel operator let a night club in the basement of the same building to use his title, the outward-appearance requirement shall be satisfied.[56)]

A majority of commentators say that a borrower shall be a merchant,[57)] contrary to a Supreme Court decision which said that a hospital can be a borrower of title.[58)]

2. Imputation

"Permission" by a name lender to use her title can either be express or tacit. But what if *X* knew that *Y* was using the trade name of *X*, but did not interfere for a long time? General opinion says that it's not sufficient. An additional factor is required, such as the permission to use her office.[59] For instance, the "imputation" requirement shall be met, if *A* and *B* engaged in the same type of business, and *A* allowed *B* to operate *B*'s business at *A*'s office.[60]

3. Good Faith

The "good faith" requirement shall be satisfied, if a third party mistakes a name lender for the operator of borrower's business. General opinion says that a third party may not be protected, if the mistake is the result of gross negligence.[61] A name lender has to prove the gross negligence of a third party to avoid the liability.[62]

C. Content of Name Lender's Liability

A name lender shall be liable jointly and severally with a borrower. A trade opponent may freely choose between a lender and a borrower to claim fulfillment of obligation. When a lender fulfills the obligation, she may claim compensation against a borrower.

A name lender shall be liable for any obligation arising out of business transactions between a borrower and a third party. A name lender is also liable for damages from the default of obligations mentioned above. In case of the rescission of contract, a name lender takes on the duty to recovery.

However, a name lender is not liable for any transactions arising out of business beyond his permission. Suppose that *X* permitted *Y* to use *X*'s name in the operation of rice mill, and that *X* rented out an attached building later. In that case *X* is not liable for any obligation arising out of the rent.[63)]

CHAPTER Ⅳ
COMMERCIAL REGISTRATION

Ⅰ. CONCEPT

Commercial registration, in Korean *sang-op-dung-gi*, means the registration of a certain matters in the commercial register in accordance with the provisions of the Commercial Act. It facilitates the safety and smoothness of trade by disclosing main facts concerning business enterprises. A ship registration under the Commercial Act Article 743 is not a commercial registration, as it is registered in the ship register, separate from the commercial register.

Provisions concerning commercial registration shall not apply to petty merchants (Commercial Act Article 9).

Ⅱ. MATTERS REQUIRING REGISTRATION

There are several matters that shall be registered under the Commercial Act. Most of them significantly affect the safety of trade. For example, we already saw that a manager "may perform all judicial and extrajudicial acts on behalf of the business proprietor, relating to her business." (Commercial Act Article 11(1)) It is very important for a trade opponent who the manager is. Thus the Commercial Act Article 13 requires a merchant to register the appointment and dismissal of a manager.

Matters requiring registration can be classified into three groups. *First*, there are matters concerning merchants in general, such as managers and trade names (Commercial Act Article 22) that we already saw. *Second*, there are matters concerning sole proprietorship only. For example, when a minor engages in any business upon the permission of his/her legal representative, registration thereof shall be required under the Commercial Act Article 6. *Third*, there are a number of matters concerning companies only, such as the establishment, dissolution and liquidation of a company.

Ⅲ. PROCEDURE

Details of the registration procedure are prescribed in the Commercial Registration Act. The Commercial Act makes only two points on the procedure: (i) matters shall be registered upon the application of a relevant party; and (ii) matters shall be registered in the commercial register of the court which has jurisdiction over the location of the applicant's business office.

The scope of reviewing authority of registration officials has been disputed. Majority of commentators say that they should examine the substantial truth of matters in the application in case of doubt.[64] However, the Supreme Court says that they need only to examine the formalities of the application.[65] The author supports the Court's opinion, as it is practically impossible for registration officials to investigate into the substantial truth of matters, even in case of doubt.[66]

Ⅳ. GENERAL EFFECTS OF REGISTRATION

A. Effect Before Registration

Matters requiring registration shall not be asserted against any third party acting in good faith unless they are registered (Commercial Act Article 37(1)). For instance, if the dismissal of a manager has not been registered, it shall not be asserted against a third party acting in good faith. However, a third party may assert a matter which is not yet registered. For example, a third party may claim invalidity of contract on the ground that the manager was dismissed.

B. Effect After Registration

Matters requiring registration can be asserted even against a third party acting in good faith, once the registration is complete (Commercial Act Article 37(1)). However, if a third party is unaware of such fact for good cause, those matters shall not be asserted against the third party, even after the registration (Article 37(2)). "Good cause" here is limited to objective ones (*e.g.* the register is destroyed in fire.). A subjective cause on the part of the third party (*e.g.* business trip or illness) shall not suffice.

Suppose that *X* is registered as a manager and *Y* is not. But *Y* fulfills the requirements for an apparent manager. *Z* concludes a contract with *Y*. Could *Z* be protected if she is acting in good faith? If the Commercial Act Article 37 applies, the third party (*Z*) shall not be protected. But the Supreme Court applies the Commercial Act Article 14, excluding Article 37, to protect a third party acting in good faith.[67)]

V. SPECIAL EFFECTS OF REGISTRATION

The registration of a certain matters may take some special effects, regardless of whether a third party is acting in good faith. These effects can be classified into three types. *First*, a new legal relationship can be established by registration. For example, a company comes into existence by the registration of establishment (Commercial Act Article 172). *Second*, one may not assert defects after registration. For instance, after the registration of a corporation's establishment, a subscriber of shares may not cancel the subscription even in case of fraud, duress or mistake (Commercial Act Article 320(1)). *Third*, certain activities may be allowed only after registration. For example, a corporation may issue share certificates only after the registration of establishment (Commercial Act Article 355).

A. Presumptive Effect of Registration?

Maybe surprisingly, commercial registration lacks public confidence, in Korean *gong-sin-ryog*.[68] It means that a person who trusted a false registration cannot be protected. Suppose that *A* was registered as manager, hired by a merchant *B*, but he is not actually one. And *X* concluded a contract with *A*, believing that *A* is truly a manager. In that case, *X* may not claim fulfillment of the contract against *B*, as the registration does not reflect the truth. It's an unfortunate consequence for a trade opponent who acted in good faith. However, as we saw earlier, the registration officials do not have the authority to investigate into the truthful fact[69]. So it's inevitable that commercial registration lacks public confidence.

Here is a small relief for a third party acting in good faith;

commercial registration has a presumptive effect, in Korean *choo-jong-ryog*. For example, if a person is registered as director or auditor of a company, he is presumed to be a legitimate director or auditor who was appointed through due process.[70] General opinion says that "presumed" here merely means a *de facto* presumption which does not shift the burden of proof.

B. Effect of False Registration

It still is a serious threat to the safety of trade that the commercial registration has only a *de facto* presumptive effect. Thus the Commercial Act Article 39 says, "No person who has intentionally or negligently registered any matter different from facts shall assert the difference against a third party acting in good faith." It is based on the principle of respect for outward appearance.

1. Prerequisites

In order to apply Article 39, the three prerequisites of the principle have to be fulfilled: (i) outward appearance, (ii) imputation and (iii) good faith.

First, the "outward appearance" requirement shall be met, when a matter that does not accord with the facts is registered. For example, a celeb was registered as director of a company, even though she was not actually appointed to the position. What if a matter was a truthful fact at the time of registration, but it became untrue due to the lack of registration for change or termination (*e.g.* registration for dismissal of a manager)? Some commentators say that both Article 37(1) and Article 39 shall apply.[71] However, Article 39 shall apply only to cases where a false information was registered in the first place.[72]

Second, the "imputation" requirement shall be safisfied, when a person intentionally or negligently registers a false information. What if a third party other than the legitimate applicant sent in a false application? Some commentators say that Article 39 shall apply even when the legitimate applicant neglected care.[73] However, Article 39 shall apply only to cases where the legitimate applicant actively engaged in false registration or knowingly let a false information get registered.[74]

Third, the "good faith" requirement shall be fulfilled, when a third party does not know that a false information was registered. If she does not know of the false registration due to gross negligence, she may not be protected.[75]

2. Effect of the Application of Article 39

When all the three requirements, described above, are met, a person who registers a false information may not assert that the registration does not accord with the facts. However, a third party may do that.

CHAPTER Ⅴ
TRANSFER OF BUSINESS

Ⅰ. CONCEPT

The transfer of business, in Korean *yong-op-yang-do*, means a contract to transfer the business assets that are integrated as an organic oneness for a certain business purpose.[76] "Assets" here include both tangible and intangible ones which have economic value, as well as negative properties, *i.e.* debts.

The key issue is whether a transferee takes over an integrated set of assets and continues to run the same business as that of a transferor.[77] If a transferor disbands a business organization and hand over all the disaggregated assets, it's not a transfer of business. If some of the assets remain in the hand of a transferor, but the business organization can be deemed to be maintained, it's a transfer of business.[78]

Ⅱ. PROCEDURE

A. Conclusion of a Contract to Transfer a Business

The transfer of business shall be made in accordance with a between a transferor and a transferee. They agree on the transfer of assets, debts, business office, trade name and employees, the price of transfer, *etc*. The contract to transfer a business is usually made in written form, even though it's not required by the Commercial Act.

B. Internal Decision-Making

In case of companies, a certain internal decision-making procedure is required. Let me take just a couple of examples concerning corporations. *First*, if a corporation is a transferor, a special resolution at the general meeting of stockholders (GMS) is required (Commercial Act Article 374(1)(i)). *Second*, if a corporation takes over a business of another company which has significant effects on the corporation, a special resolution at the GMS is also required (Commercial Act Article 374(1)(iii)).

Ⅲ. EFFECTS OF A BUSINESS TRANSFER

A. Effects Between the Parties to a Transfer

1. Duty to Hand over Business Assets

In principle a transferor shall hand over all the business assets. But some of the assets can be excluded, as long as the identity of a business can be maintained. In contrast with the succession by a universal title, such as inheritance and merger, assets shall be transferred one by one, according to the procedures prescribed by law. For instance, in case of a transfer of normative claim, in Korean *ji-myong-chae-gwon-yang-do*, a notice to or a permission by the debtor is required in order to assert the transfer against a third party.[79]

A business transfer is the transfer of an organization which is composed of both properties and personnel for a business purpose, maintaining its identity.[80] Thus, in principle, a transferee shall also succeed the labor relationship between a transferor and her employees, unless otherwise agreed.[81] But an employee may express opposite intention within a reasonable time and thereby remain in a transferor's business organization or retire from both the organizations of a transferor and a transferee.[82]

2. Non-Compete Obligation

The Commercial Act Article 41 talks about the prohibition of competition by transferor of business. The first paragraph of the article says, "When a person has transferred his or her business, he or she shall not, for a period of ten years, engage in the same kind of business in the same Special Metropolitan City, Metropolitan City, or Si/Gun, or in any adjacent Special Metropolitan City, Metropolitan City, or Si/Gun, unless the relevant parties have agreed otherwise." The geographical coverage of non-compete obligation concerns the area where a transferor's business activities have taken place, not the area where her business facilities have been located.[83)]

The second paragraph of the article goes on to say, "Where a transferor has made an agreement not to engage in the same kind of business, such agreement shall be valid, only in the same Special Metropolitan City, Metropolitan City, Si/Gun and in any adjacent Special Metropolitan City, Metropolitan City, Si/Gun, and only for a period not exceeding 20 years." There is no restraints on an agreement which reduces the geographical coverage or the period of prohibition.

B. Relationship with a Third Party

In some cases of business transfer, not all the claims and debts are handed over to a transferee. However, if the transferee continues to use the trade name of a transferor, it might appear that all the claims and debts are transferred. Thus the Commercial Act protects creditors and debtors acting in good faith, on the basis of the principle of respect for outward appearance.

1. Relationship with Creditors

a. Liability of Business Transferee Who Continues to Use Transferor's Trade Name

The Commercial Act Article 42(1) says, "If a transferee of a business continues to use the trade name of the transferor, he or she shall also be liable for repayment of the obligations of a third party arising out of the business of the transferor." A transferee's trade name doesn't have to be exactly the same as that of a transferor. It's enough that the key parts of the two trade names overlap each other, e.g. *Sam-Jong-Jang Inn* and *Sam-Jong Hotel.*[84)]

Good faith on the part of a third party is required, even though the Commercial Act does not expressly refer to it. A third party who knows of the business transfer can also be protected, if she doesn't know that an obligation to her was not transferred.[85)]

If all the requirements, described above, are met, a transferee is liable for the obligations arising out of a transferor' business. The transferee and the transferor are jointly and severally liable for the obligations.

However, there is an exception under Article 42(2). It says, "The provisions of the preceding paragraph shall not apply in cases where the transferee, without delay after the transfer of the business, registers that he or she shall not be liable for the obligations of the transferor. The same shall apply to a third party to whom both the transferor and the transferee have, without delay after the transfer of the business, given notice to the above effect and who has received such notice." It's not enough that a transferee alone gives notice to a third party.[86)]

b. Liability of Business Transferee Who Does Not Use Transferor's Trade Name

If a transferee does not use the trade name of a transferor, the outward appearance requirement is not fulfilled. Thus the transferee shall not be liable for repayment of the obligations of a third party arising out of the business of the transferor.

However, there is an exception for the principle under the Commercial Act Article 44. It says, "If, in cases where the transferee does not continue to use the transferor's trade name, he or she has made public his or her intent to assume the obligations arising out of the business of the transferor, the transferee shall also be liable to repay such obligations." The exact term "assume the obligation," or *chae-mu-in-su* in Korean, needs not be used. It's sufficient that it makes a creditor to believe the obligations are actually assumed by the transferee. Article 44 also applies when a transferee sends an individual notice to a transferor's creditor.[87)]

The Commercial Act Article 45 talks about the duration of liability of business transferor. It says, "If the transferee is liable for the obligations of the transferor in accordance with Article 42 (1) or the preceding Article, the liability of the transferor to a third party shall be extinguished two years after the transfer of the business or after the assumption of obligations is made public." Highly regarding the fact that the obligations arose out of a business, the Commercial Act gets a transferor, not the transferee, off the hook after two years.[88)]

2. Relationship with Debtors

The Commercial Act Article 43 protects a business transferor's debtor who repays to a transferee, if a transferee continues to use the trade name of a transferor. It says, "In cases falling under paragraph (1) of the preceding Article, repayment to the transferee of claims arising out of the business of the transferor shall be valid only when the obligor effecting the performance has acted in good faith and without gross negligence." If a transferee doesn't use a transferor's trade name, a transferor's creditor who repays to a transferee may not be protected.

PART IV

COMMERCIAL ACTIVITIES

CHAPTER I
COMMERCIAL AGENTS

I. CONCEPT

A commercial agent, in Korean *dae-ri-sang*, acts on behalf of a particular merchant or merchants, not as an employee, but as an agent or broker, in transactions falling within the class of business carried on by the merchant. As a commercial agent is not an employee of a merchant, but an independent merchant herself, a merchant can easily extend the geographical coverage of the business with the help of commercial agents. For example, if a merchant establishes a branch office in a new area, she has to pay all the cost, including rental cost and salaries for her employees. It could also be hard to supervise her employees from a distance. And if the business at the branch office does not go well, she has to bear all the losses. In other words, she has to bear the business risk alone. But if she concludes an agency contract with an independent merchant, the agent shall pay all the cost, including rent and salaries. Further if the merchant hire a person popular in the region, she can benefit from the agent's credit and fame. If the business thrives, the principal merchant earns the profit, and she has only to pay some commissions to the agent. If the business goes wrong, the agent, not the principal, shall bear the losses, as long as the business in the area is concerned. In short, hiring a commercial agent is much cheaper and much less risky option for a merchant than establishing her own branch office.

There are two types of commercial agents: ones with agency power and ones without it. The former, who act as an agent, can conclude a contract on behalf of the principal merchant. But the latter cannot do that. She merely acts as a broker who plans and organize deals or negotiate contracts for a commission. We call a commercial agent equipped with agency power "*che-yag-dar-ri-sang*" in Korean, and a commercial agent without agency power "*joong-gae-dae-ri-sang*" in Korean. Let us call the former a "real agent" or an "agent-agent" and the latter a "broker-agent." These titles are not official legal terms, but they could help the readers recognize more clearly the differences between the two types of commercial agents.

As broker-agents generally use the simple title of *dae-ri-sang* or *dae-ri-jom* which means an agent, it could be hard for a client to figure out whether a commercial agent has agency power or not. It can pose a serious threat to the safety of trade. Thus Article 90 of the Commercial Act allows a small exception to protect the client.

It grants a commercial agent the power to receive notices on the execution of a sales contract, even when the agent acts as a broker w/o agency power, for the convenience of the other party to a transaction. For example, a broker-agent may receive the notice of defects under Article 67(1) of the Commercial Act. Suppose that a client negotiated a deal with a broker-agent without knowing that she lacks agency power. Later when the client find-out the defect she would call the broker-agent to notify the defect rather than the principal merchant. If the broker-agent has no authority to receive the notice of defect, the notice shall be void. The client shall have to send the notice again to the principal merchant. If the client was a merchant herself, she might already have missed the chance to send immediate notice of defect. Then she may not pursue the remedies for the defected product anymore. But as the Commercial Act authorizes a broker-agent to receive the notice of defect, the notification sent to the broker-agent shall be valid and the client can pursue remedies for the defect.

Ⅱ. DUTIES OF COMMERCIAL AGENTS

A. Duty of Care of a Good Manager

We call the contract between a principal merchant and a commercial agent a "commercial agent contract." The general opinion says that a commercial agent contract is basically a delegation contract, in Korean *wi-im-gye-yak*, to which Civil Act provisions on mandate,[89] in Korean *wi-im*, shall apply. And the Supreme Court opined that a commercial agent has the duty of care of a good manager as a mandatary of the principal merchant.[90] So let's look into the concept of mandate and mandatary's duty of care of a good manager.

1. The Concept of Mandate

The Civil Act Article 680 says, "A mandate shall become effective when one of the parties has entrusted the other party with the management of affairs and the other party has consented thereto." A mandate presupposes a high level of trust between the parties, mandator, in Korean *wi-im-in*, and mandatary, in Korean *soo-im-in*. For example, a mandate relationship exists between a patient and a doctor, between a student or a student's parent and a teacher, and between a client and a lawyer. On the other hand, if a customer ordered a carpenter to build a doghouse, we call it a subcontract, in Korean *do-gup*. The carpenter needs only to build a doghouse as specified by the customer, and the contract does not presupposes such a high level of trust between the parties as a mandate relationship.

2. Mandatary's Duty of Care of a Good Manager

When a person neglects a duty of care, in Korean *joo-ui-ui-mu*, she shall be blamed for her "negligence," in Korean *gwa-sil* or *gyong-gwa-sil*. We call the severe neglect of duty of care "gross negligence," in Korean *joong-gwa-sil*. There are two types of negligence under Korean law: general negligence and individual negligence. General negligence is the neglect of the duty of care of a good manager which is generally required of a person in a particular job or position. Whereas individual negligence is the neglect of the duty of care of an individual person which is required in managing her own property.

The duty of care of a good manager is a very high level of duty, as it disregards the individual differences in ability. For example, suppose that a person asks a friend to keep her luggage without pay. According to the Civil Act Article 695 the friend shall keep the luggage with a duty of care which is required in managing her own property. If the friend kept the luggage together with her own and lost both of them, she shall not be blamed for individual negligence. But if the person pays the friend for keeping the luggage, the friend shall not be excused solely on the ground that she paid the same attention to the luggage as that of her own. If she neglected a duty of care which is generally required of a person in such a position, she shall be blamed for general negligence.

"Generally" here means that individual differences are disregarded. The concept of general negligence presupposes that a person shall be a "good manager" and she has a duty of care of a good manager. In Korean we call the duty of care of a good manager *"son-ryang-han gwan-ri-ja-ui joo-ui-ui-mu"* or *"son-gwan-ui-mu"* in short.

The duty of care of a good manager is a quite flexible concept. For example, a director of a company has a duty of care of a good manager. But a director of a small company has relatively low level of duty of care than a director of a multinational corporation.

Back to commercial agents. The Civil Act Article 681 says that a mandatary shall have the duty of care of a good manager, and, according to the Supreme Court decision mentioned above, the article shall apply to commercial agents. Thus commercial agents have the duty of care of a good manager, a very high level of duty of care under Korean law.

The Commercial Act imposes additional duties on commercial agents that the Civil Act does not impose on mandataries. They are:

- Duty to notify transactions
- Non-compete obligation
- Duty to keep trade secret

Let's investigate them one by one.

B. Duty to Notify Transactions

I told you earlier that a student's parent and a teacher are in a mandate relationship[91]. How often shall a teacher report to the parent about her student's progress? Once a week? Once a month? Or every day? The Civil Act Article 683 talks about a mandatary's duty to report. It says, "A mandatary shall upon demand by the mandator report on the status of the management of the entrusted affairs, and upon the termination of the mandate he shall make a full report on the entire developments with respect to the management of the entrusted affairs without delay." It means that a teacher shall report to the parent when the parent ask for it, and when she quits teaching the student. In other words the Civil Act does not require the mandatary to report to the mandator regularly or frequently. If the mandator does not request for an interim report, the mandatary does not have to report at all, as long as she keeps teaching. Of course, teachers usually report to the parents quite regularly, especially after exams. But it's not a legal duty.

However, the Commercial Act puts much heavier burden of report upon commercial agents. Article 88 says, "When a commercial agent has acted as agent or broker in any transaction, he or she shall give a notice thereof to the principal without delay." It means that a commercial agent has to report to the principal merchant immediately, whenever she makes a deal on behalf of the principal (if she is a real agent) or mediates between the principal and a client (if she is just a broker-agent without agency power). It could be facsimile or email or intranet report. In any method agreed between the agent and the principal, the agent has to report to the principal right after she makes a deal or mediates between the parties.

C. Non-Compete Obligation

Earlier we discussed the duty of commercial employees under Article 17 of the Commercial Act[92]. You might recall that it has two parts: non-compete obligation and dual office ban. The Commercial Act Article 89 prescribes similar duty of commercial agents. But there are some differences between the wording of Articles 17 and 89.

Let's first look at the similarities. *First*, the two articles have the same structure. Article 89 also consists of two parts: non-compete obligation and dual office ban. *Second*, the non-compete-obligation part of the two articles are identical. Article 89(1) says, "Without the permission of the principal, a commercial agent shall not make, on his or her own account or for a third party, any transaction in the same type of business as the principal, or serve as general partner or a director of a company whose purpose is to engage in the same kind of business of the principal." Just like a commercial employee, a commercial agent shall not engage in a business in competition with her principal merchant without the permission of the latter. *Third*, remedies are the same under the two articles, as Article 89(2) applies mutatis mutandis Article 17(2), (3) and (4). That is, in case of the breach of Article 89(1), a principal merchant may terminate the contract, claim damages against the commercial agent and/or exert a right to intervention.

Next, the differences. *First*, under Article 17 a commercial employee shall not become a general partner or a director of a company, even when the company's business is not in competition with that of the principal merchant. But under Article 89 a commercial agent shall not work for a company only when it is a competitor of the principal. *Second*, Article 17 prohibits a commercial employee from serving as an employee of another merchant. But Article 89 is silent on this issue. Despite the silence, a majority of commentators say that a commercial agent shall not serve as an employee of another merchant, either.[93)]

D. Duty to keep trade secret

We already saw that a commercial agent is a mandatary and has the duty of care of a good manger under the Civil Act. In other words, a commercial agent has to be a good manager. As a good manager, a commercial agent shall keep the secrets of a principal.

It seems that we don't need any additional provision on the duty of commercial agent to keep trade secret. But the Commercial Act has one. Why? Because it is not evident whether a commercial agent has to keep the trade secret, *after* the term of a commercial agent contract. During the contracted period, the Civil Act provisions on mandate shall apply to a commercial agent. But after the period of the contract, the *former* commercial agent is not a mandatary anymore. Thus in 1995 the Commercial Act introduced Article 92-3 to make sure that a commercial agent shall keep the trade secrets of the principal even after the contract is terminated.

Ⅲ. RIGHTS OF COMMERCIAL AGENTS

A. Lien

Earlier we saw the two types of real security: pledge and mortgage[94)]. In case of pledge and mortgage, the security right holders have the right to preferential payment. For example, suppose that *A* borrowed some money from *B*, and *B* held *A*'s laptop in pledge to secure the debt. If *A* fails to pay the money back in time, *B* may sell the laptop in auction and get her money back from the auction price, before other creditors get their shares. Likewise, if *B* held mortgage on *A*'s house, *B* may sell it by auction, and get her money back from the auction price, prior to other creditors without security right. That's the right to preferential payment of a security right holder.

Now, let us add another type of real security: lien, in Korean *yoo-chi-gwon*. The Civil Act Article 320 says, "If the possessor of a thing or valuable instruments belonging to another person has any claim arising, in respect of such property or instruments and if payment of the claim is due, he may retain possession of the thing or instruments until the claim is satisfied." For example, if *X* repaired *Y*'s watch upon *Y*'s request, *X* may keep the watch in his custody, until *Y* pays the repair cost. A lien holder does not have the right to preferential payment. However, when a creditor hold a lien on a stuff, he can retain the stuff until he gets the money back. Thus a lien can be a very strong security right, even without the right to preferential payment.

The lien under the Civil Act is itself a powerful security right. But the Commercial Act grants a bit more powerful lien to a commercial agent. Under the Civil Act, a certain relationship should exist between the debt and the stuff on which the creditor holds lien: the claim has to arise in respect of the stuff. For example, the watch and the repair cost in our case fulfills the requirement. However, the Commercial Act grants lien to a commercial agent even without such a requirement. The main sentence of Article 91 says, "A commercial agent may retain goods or securities which he or she holds in his or her possession on behalf of the principal, in respect of the obligations which have arisen from his or her agency or brokerage in transactions and which have become due, until he or she receives repayment of such obligations." Suppose that *A* is a commercial agent, and *B* is her principal merchant. *A* sold a refrigerator on behalf of *B*, but *B* did not pay the fee for the sale. *A* holds possession of a washing machine that she is going to sell on behalf of *B*. The washing machine and the fee for the sale of a refrigerator have nothing to do with each other. But, under the Commercial Act Article 91, *A* may hold lien on the washing machine, until she gets the fee for the sale of a refrigerator. As it could be a little too harsh for the principal merchant, the proviso of the article allows an exception when there is any different agreement between the parties.

B. Right of Claim for Fee

The Commercial Act Part 2 Chapter 2, entitled "Commercial Agents", does not have any provision on commercial agents' right of claim for fee. But a commercial agent may demand remuneration under Article 61 that we already saw. Under the article, a merchant may demand a fee for her effort, if she did anything for other person within the scope of her business. You might recall the slogan, "No free lunch with a merchant." As a commercial agent is a merchant herself, she may demand the remuneration for her effort under the article, when she concludes a contract on behalf of the principal or mediates between the principal and another party.

C. Right of Claim for Compensation

Suppose that *A* is a principal and *B* is a commercial agent in the city of *X*. *B* is a popular person in the area and worked very hard for *A*. Thanks to the effort, *A*'s brand sold well in the city *X*. But then *A* terminated the contract with *B*, and established her own branch office. The business is still thriving. Could *B* demand any compensation for her effort after the termination of contract? Well, as we just saw, *B* may demand remuneration for her effort during the contract period under Article 61. However, it's not clear whether she may do that even after the termination of contract. Thus in 1995 the Commercial Act introduced Article 92-2 to make sure that a commercial agent may claim for compensation, even after the termination of contract. In order for a commercial agent to claim for compensation, three requirements have to be met under the article: (i) the principal obtains new customers or her business transaction has increased remarkably through the commercial agent's activities; (ii) the principal gains thereby profits even after the contract is terminated; and (iii) the contract is not terminated by any reason attributable to the commercial agent. When all the requirements are met the commercial agent may claim a reasonable compensation.

However, the Commercial Act puts a cap on the amount of compensation here. Article 92-2(2) says, "The amount of compensation pursuant to paragraph (1) may not exceed the average annual remuneration for the last five years before the contract is terminated. If the term of the contract is less than five years, it shall be based on the average annual remuneration for such period." In addition Article 92-2(3) puts a time limit on the claim for compensation: a commercial agent shall have to claim compensation under Article 92-2(1) within 6 months after the termination of contract.

CHAPTER Ⅱ COMMERCIAL BROKERS

Ⅰ. CONCEPT

Now we turn to another type of the outside helpers of merchants: commercial brokers, in Korean *joong-gae-sang*. Commercial brokers mediate between the parties in commercial transactions. Just like commercial agents, they are independent merchants themselves. But they act just as a broker. Unlike broker-agents that we just saw, there is no discordance between their title and competence. They don't sound like an agent, and they don't have any agency power. Is it a bad thing that they lack agency power? Not always so. As they are not an agent of any one of the parties, they could play an important role as a *neutral* third party. Their neutral position can help the clients make a deal through. Besides commercial agents assist merchants by looking for clients, investigating into their credibility and providing information on markets and trades.

The Commercial Act Article 93 defines a commercial broker as "a person who engages in the business of acting as an intermediary in commercial activities between other persons." Here let's look at the following two elements of the concept more closely.

First, "commercial activities" here include both unilateral and reciprocal ones. You recall that a unilateral commercial activity is a transaction where only one of the parties is a merchant and a reciprocal commercial activity is a transaction where both of the parties are merchant. Thus a commercial broker mediates a transaction not only between merchants, but also between a merchant and a non-merchant. However, if a broker mediates between non-merchants, she is not a commercial broker, but a civil broker. For example, a marriage broker is a civil broker. A civil broker is also a merchant under Article 46(xi), and the common provisions on commercial activities (Commercial Act Part 2 Chapter 1) apply to them. But the Commercial Act provisions on brokerage (Part 2 Chapter 6) apply only to commercial brokers.

Second, "other persons" in Article 93 indicates many and unspecified persons. Whereas, in case of broker-agents, they act as a broker of a particular merchant (Article 87). Broker-agents may work only for specified merchants. But commercial brokers may work for many and unspecified clients.

Ⅱ. DUTIES OF COMMERCIAL BROKERS

There are diverging views on the characterization of a brokerage contract between a commercial agent and her client.[95] But this book characterizes it as a delegation contract, unless otherwise agreed between the parties. Thus, in principle, a commercial agent is a mandatary and has the duty of care of a good manager under the Civil Act Article 681. We don't have to repeat the details on the duty of care of a good manager here. The Commercial Act imposes additional duties on commercial brokers. Let's look into those additional duties one by one.

A. Duty to Keep Samples

When a lady visits a cosmetics shop, she used to get some complimentary samples. They are free giveaways at her disposal. But merchants sometimes send samples to the buyers in order to guarantee the quality of their products. In that case those samples need to be retained in preparation for a dispute on the quality of products. Thus the Commercial Act Article 95 says, "If a broker has received a sample in connection with an activity in which he or she has acted as an intermediary, he shall keep custody of such sample until the completion of the said activity." Article 95 applies only to sales of products, the quality of which is guaranteed by a sample. The main purpose of the article is to prepare for disputes on the defects of products. Thus a broker shall keep samples until there is no prospect of such disputes any more, even after the mediation is completed.

B. Duty to Deliver Contract Documents

A contract indicates an agreement between the parties. It can be made orally, but often it is evidenced in writing. In the latter case, a document is drawn up to contain the terms of contract and the signatures of both parties. We call this document "a contractual document," in Korean *gye-yak-so*, or simply a contract. But Article 96 talks about a whole new type of document, "a contract document," in Korean *gyol-yak-so*, which is totally different from a contract or a contractual document. As soon as a transaction has been made between the parties, a commercial broker shall draw up contract documents which contain the name or trade name of each party, the date and a summary of the contract (Article 96(1)). A contract document is just an evidence of a contract drawn up to prevent disputes between the parties. If the parties did not draw up a contractual document, the contract document could be a written evidence of the term of contract. If a contractual document is falsified by a party, the contract document could help the court to find out the original term of contract. A contract document is neither a contract itself nor a prerequisite for a contract. Thus a contract can be valid, even if a commercial agent does not draw up a contract document.

The commercial broker shall first sign the contract documents or fix her seal on them (Article 96(1)). Then she shall deliver them to each party to have them sign the documents or fix their seals on them (Article 96(2)). If any of the parties refuses to accept the documents, write her name and sign them or affix her seal on thcm, the commercial broker shall immediately notify it to the other party (Article 96(3)). If a broker fails to send the notice immediately, the other party can claim damages against her. When a contract document is completed, it shall contain the signature of both parties and the commercial broker. On the other hand a contract shall contain only the signature of both parties.

C. Duty to Maintain Books

Suppose that a dispute arose between the parties *A* and *B* on the term of contract. They did not draw up a contractual document, and *A* lost her copy of contract document. *B* produced her own copy of contract document as evidence, but *A* believes that it was falsified. How could *A* prove the original term of contract? To prepare for a situation like this, Article 97(1) demands the commercial broker to keep record of the content of contract documents in her books. Books here are called "broker's diary." They shall be maintained as evidence of trade between the parties. Thus either party may at any time demand the broker to deliver a copy of her books in connection with the activity in which the broker has acted as intermediary for the party (Article 97(2)).

D. Duty to Maintain the Anonymity of Parties

In commercial transactions, anonymity often can give advantage to a party, while the other party might not care much about her identity. Thus the Commerical Act Article 98 imposes on a commercial broker a duty not to disclose the name or trade name of a party who requests for anonymity. As we just saw, the name or trade name of each party can be revealed to the other party in two types of documents: contract documents and a copy of broker's diary. A commercial broker shall not enter the name or trade name of anonymous party in any one of those documents that are to be delivered to the other party. The party who entrusted mediation to a broker may, of course, demand anonymity. But the other party also may do that. In any case the broker shall not disclose the name or trade name of an anonymous party to the other party.

E. Duty to Guarantee Contract Fulfillment

In case of anonymity of a party, the Commercial Act Article 99 imposes a duty to guarantee contract fulfillment on the broker to protect the other party who trusted her. If it were not for the provision, the other party shall not be able to claim contract fulfillment against the commercial broker, as the broker is neither a party nor an agent of a party to the contract. The article applies not only to a situation where one of the parties demanded anonymity, but also where the commercial broker voluntarily has not disclosed the name or trade name of a party. Once a broker owes a duty to guarantee contract fulfillment, the duty shall not be terminated, even if she discloses the name or trade name of the anonymous party later.

The duty is called "intervention duty". But it should be noted that, in case of intervention, a broker does not become a party to a transaction. After fulfilling a contract on behalf of a party, the broker can just claim for reimbursement against her.

Ⅲ. RIGHT OF COMMERCIAL BROKERS

A. Right to Demand Remuneration

Although the Commercial Act Article 61 already talks about a merchant's right of claim for fee, the Act has a special provision on the right of commercial agents to demand remuneration. Article 100(1) says that a commercial broker shall not demand remuneration unless he has complied with the formalities prescribed in Article 96. In other words, a commercial broker may demand remuneration only after she completes the contract documents, delivers them to each party and, if any one of the parties refuses to accept and sign them, notifies it to the other party.

The Commercial Act Article 100(2) says that the broker's remuneration shall be borne by both parties in equal proportions. Thus a commercial agent may not demand any one of the parties to pay the portion borne by the other party. It is generally interpreted that Article 100(2) shall not apply when a special agreement or custom provides otherwise.

B. Lack of Right to Receive Payment or Other Provision

A commercial broker does not have the right to receive payment or other provision, as she is neither a party nor an agent of a party to a transaction. But the Commercial Act Article 94 allows an exception when a special agreement or custom provides otherwise. If one of the parties remains anonymous upon her demand, it could be assumed that there is a tacit agreement to invest the broker a right to receive payment or other provision.

CHAPTER III COMMISSION AGENTS

Ⅰ. CONCEPT

A. Definition

The Commercial Act Article 101 defines a commission agent, in Korean *wi-tak-mae-mae-in*, as “a person who makes it his or her business to effect sale and purchase of goods or securities under his or her own name on the account of another party.” To understand the concept of commission agent, let’s think about the relationship between a publisher and a book store.

Suppose that a book store ordered 50 volumes of new novel issued by a publisher. The book store hoped that the book will be a million seller. But, contrary to the expectation, the bookstore sold only one volume. It became evident that she won’t be able to sell any more volume. Now what should she do with the remaining 49 volumes? Should she sell them as waste paper, or return it to the publisher? Yes, you’re right. The book store may return the volumes to the publisher. But what exactly do you mean by “return” here? Do you mean “resell”? In other words, do you mean that the book store earlier bought the volumes from the publisher and now resell them to the publisher?

Not exactly so. On the surface the ownership of the books were transferred from the publisher to the book store, so that the book store could sell them to the customers. When the book store sells a volume to a customer, the book store becomes a party to the sales contract. In other words she conclude a contract in her own name. Thus all the rights and duties stemming from the contract belong to her. However, under the surface, the books still belong to the publisher. The book store sells them on the account of the publisher. Thus all the profit and loss stemming from the sale belong to the publisher. For example, when the book store sells a volume and a customer pay the price to the book store, she shall send the money to the publisher. Then the publisher shall pay some commission to the book store. Basically the publisher is the one who earns money from the sale. On the contrary, if the book doesn't sell, the book store may return the volumes to the publisher. Then the publisher shall bear all the loss. Here a separation of legal consequences and economic consequences occurred. This type of transaction, in which the separation of economic and legal consequences occurs, is called *"joo-son"* in Korean. When a person sells or buys a stuff in *joo-son* style, that is, in her own name and on the account of other person, we call her a commission agent.

In the past commission agents greatly helped merchants in

developing new markets in foreign countries, as the merchants could rely on the reputation and credit of commission agents in those countries. Thanks to the development of broadcasting and telecommunication, merchants do not have to rely on commission agents as much as before. But commission agents are still playing an important role in various areas, such as the markets for negotiable instruments, agricultural products and antiques.

B. Comparison

A commission agent is a merchant herself who assists other merchant from outside, just like a commercial agent and a commercial broker. But there are several differences between those merchants. *First*, a commission agent becomes a party to the contract that she arranges for the principal, so that all the rights and duties stemming from the contract belong to her. But a commercial agent without agency power, *i.e.* a broker-agent, and a commercial broker simply mediates between the parties, without being a party. *Second*, a commission agent concludes a contract in her own name. But a commercial agent equipped with agency power, *i.e.* an agent-agent, concludes a contract in the name of principal so that the principal shall become a party to the contract. In other words, in cases of an agent-agent, the agent does not become a party, and all the rights and duties stemming from the contract belong to the principal.

As we saw earlier, a commission agent concludes a sales contract in *joo-son* style[96]. But there are two more types of *joo-son* under the Commercial Act. When a person concludes a carriage contract in her own name and on the account of other person, she is called a transportation broker. The Commercial Act has a separate chapter on transportation brokers. But the Commercial Act Article 123 applies *mutatis mutandis* some of the provisions on commission agents to transportation brokers. When a person concludes a contract other than sales and carriage contract, *e.g.* an advertisement contract, she is called a quasi-commission agent. The Commercial Act Article 113 applies *mutatis mutandis* the provisions on commission agents to quasi-commission agents.

Ⅱ. EXTERNAL RELATIONSHIP

We already saw that a separation of economic and legal consequences occurs, when a commission agent concludes a contract on behalf of the principal. Let's focus on the legal consequences here. The Commercial Act Article 102 says, "By a sale or purchase made on behalf of another party, the commission agent directly acquires rights and assumes obligations with regard to the other party to the transaction." To understand what it means, let me take two examples. *First*, suppose that a book store sells a volume to a customer. But two pages were missing in the volume. In other words, it has a defect. Now the customer wants some remedy for the defect. Who should she call, the publisher or the book store? Usually the customer who bought a volume with a defect would call the book store. And it's the right answer even from a legal perspective. As all the rights and duties stemming from the sale belong to the book store (a commission agent), she shall take on the legal responsibility for the defect. But, of course, as all the profit and loss from the sale belong to the publisher (a principal), ultimately the publisher shall provide a volume without defect. *Second*, suppose that a book store sold a volume to a customer on credit. But she would not pay the price, even when it's overdue. For some reason the book store is hesitant to claim damages against the customer. Could the publisher claim damages against the customer? The answer is negative. Because all the rights and duties stemming from the sale belong to the book store, the publisher may not directly claim damages against the customer. The publisher may just call the book store to account under the Commercial Act Article 105 that we will look into later[97]. In other words, in an external relationship between the book store and the customer, the publisher is a total stranger who has no say in the matter.

But, in the internal relationship between the publisher and the book store, things are quite different. The ownership of the volumes belongs to the publisher in the internal relationship, whereas the ownership belongs to the book store in the external relationship with a customer. The book store has to first acquire the ownership so that she could later transfer it to the customer. Here a separation of formality and substance occurs. In formality the book belongs to the book store, while in substance it belongs to the publisher. In the external relationship with a customer, only the formality counts. A book store may sell a volume to a customer, as if she is the true owner of the volume. But in the internal relationship, they shall return to the substance. The book store cannot claim the ownership against the publisher.

However, the dichotomy of internal and external relationship is not a cure-all. Suppose that a book store *X* borrowed some money from a creditor *Y*. *X* failed to pay the money back in time. *Y* is trying to seize the properties of *X* to get her money back. Could *Y* seize the volumes on the book shelf of *X* that were provided by a publisher *Z* under a commission agent contract? If we mechanically apply the dichotomy, it's an external relationship issue and the ownership of the volumes belong to *X*. So *Y* may seize the volumes to get her money back. But the outcome is certainly unacceptable, as it collides with the substance of a commission agent contract. Thus the Commercial Act allows an exception to the dichotomy: in the external relationship between a principal and the creditor of a commission agent, the ownership of goods consigned belongs to the principal.

Summing up the above discussion, the Commercial Act Article 103 talks about the ownership of goods consigned as follows: "Goods or securities received by the commission agent from his or her principal, or goods, securities or claims acquired through a sale or purchase by the commission agent, are deemed to belong to the principal so far as the principal and the commission agent or the principal and the commission agent's creditor are concerned."

Ⅲ. DUTIES OF COMMISSION AGENTS

Now let's look more closely into the internal relationship between a commission agent and a principal. It can be described with the rights and duties of commission agents. Let's start from the duties.

A. Duty of Care of a Good Manager

Unlike in the case of commercial agents, the Commercial Act Article 112 expressly provides that the provisions on mandate under the Civil Act shall apply to the relations between a principal and a commission agent. Thus a commission agent has the duty of care of a good manager as a mandatary. As we already talk about the duty several times, we don't need to repeat it here again. Let's move on to investigate the additional duties that the Commercial Act imposes on a commission agent.

B. Duty to Notify a Sale or Purchase and to Submit Statement of Account

Earlier we saw that the Commercial Act Article 88 imposes a duty to notify on commercial agents which is heavier than mandatary's duty to report under the Civil Act[98]. But Article 104 of the Act imposes even heavier duty on commission agents. It says, "If a commission agent has effected a sale or purchase consigned to him or her, he or she shall send notice of a summary of the contract and of domicile and the full name of the other party, and he or she shall submit the statement of account thereof to his or her principal without delay." You may notice two differences between Articles 88 and 104. *First*, Article 104 specifies some details that have to be included in the notice to a principal: a summary of contract and of domicile and full name of the other partner. *Second*, Article 104 adds a duty to submit statement of account. As a principal does not become a party to a contract that a commission agent concludes on behalf of the principal, the Commercial Act demands the commission agent to send notice in some more details and submit the statement of account to the principal.

C. Duty to Observe Designated Price

Suppose that *X* is a rich person who wants to buy an antique, say a *Yi Dynasty* porcelain, or *Yi-Jo-Baek-Ja* in Korean. She asks a commission agent *A* to buy one at a price lower than KRW 100 million. *A* finds that *Y* has one and negotiates with him only to find that he wants to sell it at least for KRW 120 million. If *A* buys it from *Y* at the price of KRW 120 million, should *X* accept the deal? Obviously *A* fails to meet the price designated by *X*, which is KRW 100 million, and the deal shall not bind be binding upon *X*. Thus *X* may reject the deal and doesn't have to pay commission to *A*.

But what if *A* fills the gap between the designated price and the actual price? If *A* receives KRW 100 million from *X* and add her own money, KRW 20 million, and then pays KRW 120 million in total to *Y* for the antique, could *X* still reject the deal? As *X* bears no loss in this case, she may not reject the deal and *A* can claim for commission against *X*. But you might wonder why *A* would endure the loss by putting her own money into the deal. Well, merchants sometimes take short term loss for long term gain. For example, if *X* plans to buy several antiques to decorate her new home, *A* might be willing to put her own money to get the first deal through so that she could receive further orders from *X*.

The same principles apply to a reverse situation. Suppose that *Y* asks a commission agent *A* to sell a *Yi Dynasty* porcelain at a price higher than KRW 120 million. If *A* sells the antique for only KRW 100 million to *X*, *Y* may reject the deal and *A* cannot claim for commission against *Y*. But if *A* fills the gap of KRW 20 million with her own money, then *Y* may not reject the deal and *A* can claim for commission.

The Commercial Act Article 106(1) beautifully summarizes the above principles: "If a commission agent has sold goods, *etc*. at a lower price or bought them at a higher price than the price designated by his or her principal and the commission agent bears the difference, the sale or purchase shall be binding upon the principal." When a commission agent fails to meet a designated price, a consignor may reject the transaction, as it runs counter to the main purpose of consignment. However, if the commission agent bears the difference, the Commercial Act allows her to claim for fee against the consignor, as the latter does not suffer any loss.

Now further suppose that *X* asks a commission agent *A* to buy a *Goryeo* celadon, or *Go-Ryo-Chong-Ja* in Korean, at the price of KRW 200 million. If *A* successfully negotiated with *Y* and buys the item from him for only KRW 150 million, could *A* send only KRW 150 million to *Y* and get the profit of KRW 50 million? You recall that a commission agent buys or sells stuffs for the account of a consignor. It means that all the economic consequences belong to a consignor, not to a commission agent. So, in this case, the profit should go to *X*, not *A*.

The same principle applies to a reverse situation. Suppose that *Y* asks a commission agent *A* to sell a Goryeo celadon at the price of KRW 200 million, but *A* sells it to *X* for KRW 250 million. *A* may not get the profit and should send all KRW 250 million to *Y*. *A* can only claim for commission against *Y*.

Again he Commercial Act Article 106(2) neatly summarizes the principle: "When a commission agent has sold goods, *etc*. at a higher price or bought them at a lower price than the price designated by his or her principal, the difference shall be deemed to be profits of the principal unless otherwise agreed by the parties." In other words, when a commission agent conducts sales/ purchase at a better price than a designated one, the profit shall go to a consignor, as the transaction is conducted for the account of the latter.

D. Liability to Secure Performance

Suppose that a commission agent concluded a contract with *X* to buy a stuff for her client *Y*. If *X* does not perform the contractual obligation, *Y* may not directly claim contract fulfillment against *X*, as she is not a party to the transaction. Thus Article 105 of the Commercial Act imposes a duty to guarantee contract fulfillment on a commission agent to protect her client. The main sentence of the article says, "If the other party does not perform obligations arising from a sale or purchase which a commission agent has effected for his or her principal, the commission agent shall be liable for the performance thereof." In our case above, if *X* does not perform the contractual obligation, *A* has to fulfill the contract. However, this shall not apply if a commission agent and his principle agreed otherwise, or if there is a special custom (Proviso of Article 105).

E. Duty to Notify Damage, *etc.*

When a commission agent becomes aware of, after having acquired the subject matter of the sale through a commission agency, any damage or defect in the goods, or there is a fear of decomposition or decay of the goods, or commercial circumstances which show decline of commodity prices, he shall without delay send a notice thereof to his principal (Commercial Act Article 108(1)). If the commission agent is unable to receive the instruction of his principal or such instruction is delayed, the commission agent may take an adequate measure for the benefit of his principal (Commercial Acat Article 108(2)).

Ⅲ. RIGHTS OF COMMISSION AGENTS

A. Right to Claim the Reimbursement of Costs

Under the Civil Act a commission agent is a mandatary and her client is a mandator. Article 687 of the Civil Act talks about mandatary's right to demand payment of expenses in advance: "If any expense is required for the management of the entrusted affairs, the mandator shall, upon demand by the mandatary, pay them in advance." Article 688(1) of the Civil Act also talks about mandatary's right to demand reimbursement of expenses, *etc.*: "Where a mandatary has defrayed any expenses incurred in management of the entrusted affairs, he or she may demand from the mandator the reimbursement of such expenses with interest thereon from the day they were defrayed." Thus a commission agent has a right to claim reimbursement of costs against her client under those provisions.

B. Right to Claim for Fee

As we saw earlier, a merchant has a right to demand remuneration under Article 61 of the Commercial Act[99]. A commission agent is a merchant and she can claim for fee against her client under the article.

C. Lien

Earlier we looked into the Commercial Act Article 91 which talks about the lien of commercial agents[100]. The Commercial Act Article 111 applies Article 91 *mutatis mutandis* (*i.e.* with some necessary changes) to a commission agent. Thus a commercial agent may retain goods or securities which he holds in his possession on behalf of the principal, in respect of the obligations which have arisen from his sales or purchases and which have become due, until he receives repayment of such obligations.

D. Right to Intervention

When a commission agent has received a commission to sell or purchase goods or negotiable instruments, which has the exchange quotation, there is no concern on conflicting interest between a commission agent and a consignor regarding the price. Thus the Commercial Act Article 107 invests the former with a right to intervention so that a commission agent may directly become the buyer or seller. In such a case the price shall be determined by exchange quotation at the time when notice of sale or purchase was dispatched by the commission agent (Article 107(1)). A commission agent may claim for fee against her client, even when she exerts the right to intervention (Article 107(2)).

CHAPTER IV CARRIAGE

Ⅰ. CONCEPT

A carrier, in Korean *oon-song-in*, assists merchants in coping with the geographical limitations on their business activities. Suppose that a crab is sold at a relatively low price in a coastal area. But it can be sold at a higher price in a big city away from the coast. A carrier can help a merchant, who sells crabs, to earn a bigger amount of money by transporting crabs from a village of coast to a metropolitan area.

There are three types of carriage, in Korean *oon-song*, according to the place where the transportation is carried out: land carriage, carriage by sea and air transport. Part II of the Commercial Act allots only a chapter to land carriage (Chapter V). But the Act allots a whole part to carriage by sea (Part V) and another to air transport (Part VI), as they entail much greater risks than land carriage. Here in this book we will focus only on land carriage. So, hereinafter, when we say simply "carriage" or "carrier", it means land carriage or land carrier.

The Commercial Act Chapter V on land carriage starts from

Article 125 which defines a carrier. It says, "For the purposes of this Act, the term "carrier" means a person who engages in the business of carrying goods or passengers by land or on lakes and rivers, and in ports and bays." We can see that a carrier transports not only goods but also passengers. "Goods" here include everything that can be an object of transportation and custody, and they do not have to be an object of transaction (*e.g.* bodies). "Passengers" here include all the natural persons, and they do not have to be a party to a carriage contract (*e.g.* children). "By land" here means over ground (*e.g.* bus, taxi, truck and train) and underground (*e.g.* metro). Land carriage under the Commercial Act includes carriages on lakes/rivers and in ports/bays, as their scale is relatively small and they entail similar degree of risks as carriage by land.

A carriage contract is essentially a contract for work, in Korean *do-gub-gye-yak*, as its objective is to complete a work.[101] The Civil Act has several provisions on a contract for work, including Article 664 which defines it. The article says, "A contract for work becomes effective when one of the parties has agreed to perform a certain job and the other has agreed to pay remuneration for the result of such work." However, the Civil Act provisions on a contract for work[102] hardly applies to a carriage contract, as the Commercial Act contains many detailed provisions on it.

Ⅱ. CARRIERS' LIABILITIES FOR DAMAGES

Now let us examine a case on a carrier's liability for damages. A carrier here means, of course, a land carrier.

> **[CASE]** Rebecca bought a pair of high-end shoes at the price of KRW 1 million in Seoul, planning to resell it to a person in Tokyo at the price of KRW 1.5 million. She sent those shoes to her office in Busan through a carrier. But she packed them in a shabby box and did not tell the carrier about their price. Receiving the package, Rebecca found the shoes severely damaged beyond repair. Could Rebecca claim damages against the carrier? If positive, what shall be the amount of damages?

A. Issues

The case involves several issues as follows: (i) cause of liability, (ii) amount of damages, and (iii) liability for valuables. Let's look into them one by one.

B. Cause of Liability

When Rebecca tries to claim damages against the carrier, he might respond that the package was already damaged when he received it. Or he might insist that it's not his fault and he won't compensate for the damages unless Rebecca produces evidence that it's his fault. Should Rebecca produce evidence that it's the carrier's fault? Or should the carrier provide evidence that it's not his fault? We call this type of issue the burden of proof. If the carrier has the burden of proof, he should provide evidence to avoid the liability. But if Rebecca has the burden, they should produce evidence to claim damages against the carrier. Before we look at the commercial law principles on the issue, let's first look at the civil law principles.

Under the Civil Act, a debtor shall be liable for the default caused by the negligence of his assistant, and, to avoid the liability, he has to prove that the assistant did not neglected care (Civil Act Article 391). But, in the case of torts or illegal activities (Civil Act Article 750), in Korean *bool-bop-haeng-wi*, the burden of proof shall be placed on the victim. In a contractual relationship, a debtor is expected to fulfill the contractual obligation. When he fails to do that, he has to prove that it's not his fault to avoid the liability. But in case of torts, there is no such expectation, and the victim has to provide the evidence of wrongdoer's fault or willfulness.

A carrier and his client are in a contractual relationship. Thus, if a carrier fails to fulfill the contractual obligation to transport a package without any loss, injury or delay, he shall have the burden of proof. That is, in order to avoid the liability, he has to provide evidence that the loss, injury or delay was not his fault. That's exactly what the Commercial Act prescribes. Article 135 of the Act says, "A carrier shall be liable for damage resulting from the loss of, damage to or delay in the delivery of goods unless he or she proves that the carrier, forwarding agents, his or her employees, or other persons employed in respect of the carriage did not fail to exercise due care in connection with the receipt, delivery, custody, and carriage of the goods." In other words, a carrier is liable for the damages only when he or his performance assistant, in Korean *i-haeng-bo-jo-ja*, intentionally or negligently caused the damages. In order to avoid the liability, a carrier has to prove that neither he nor his assistant neglected care. It is not enough to prove that he did not neglected care in hiring and supervising the assistant.

Just like the Civil Act Article 391, the Commercial Act Article 135 is based on the principle of liability with fault, in Korean *gwa-sil-chaeg-im-ju-ui*, and the burden of proof is placed on the debtor, *i.e.* the carrier. Thus general opinion says that the Commercial Act Article 135 is not an exception to the general rules under the Civil Act, but just puts the rules into shape concerning carriage.

C. Amount of Damages

When a carrier fails to prove that neither he nor his assistant neglected care, then the carrier is liable for the damages. But then the next issue arises: the amount of damages. For example, in our case, should the carrier pay the damage of KRW 1 million or KRW 1.5 million? Once again, let's first look at the civil law principles on the issue, and then investigate the commercial law principles.

The Civil Act Article 393(1) says, "The compensation for damages arising from the non-performance of an obligation shall be limited to ordinary damages." "Ordinary damages," in Korean *tong-sang-son-hae*, here means damages in proximate causal relation, in Korean *sang-dang-in-gwa-gwan-gye*, with the non-performance of obligation. For example, when a stuff is damaged beyond repair, the price of the stuff shall be the ordinary damages. Ordinary damages are also called usual damages.

The Civil Act Article 393(2) goes on to say, "The obligor is responsible for reparation for damages that have arisen through special circumstances, only if he had foreseen or could have foreseen such circumstances." It talks about unusual (special) damages, in Korean *took-byol-son-hae*, that are not in proximate causal relation with the non-performance of obligation. For instance, when a buyer planned to resell a stuff at profit, the trading profit or margin shall be the unusual (special) damages. But the debtor is liable for those damages, only when he had actually foreseen or could have foreseen the special circumstances.

The Commercial Act standardizes the amount of damages concerning carriage in two ways. *First*, the Act says that the amount of damages shall be determined only by the price of package. *Second*, it designates the time place which shall be the basis to determine the price. Article 137(1) of the Act says, "If transported goods have been totally lost or their delivery has been delayed, the amount of damages shall be determined by the price prevailing at the place of destination on the day they should have been delivered." And Article 137(2) goes on to say, "In cases of a partial loss of or damage to goods, the amount of damages shall be determined by the price prevailing at the place of destination on the date of delivery."

These measures dramatically mitigate the liability of carriers and protect them from the disputes on damages. For example, in our case, the carrier does not have to worry about the unusual damages, *i.e.* the trading profit that Rebecca planned to make. He needs only to pay the usual damages, *i.e.* the price of those shoes. Also the carrier does not have to worry about the disputes on the time and place to determine the price, as the Act already designates them in detail. If it were not for the Commercial Act Article 137, carriers might suffer frequent disputes on the time and place to determine the price, as the price varies according to time and place. As carriers usually transport hundreds of thousands of packages every day, the special rules under the Commercial Act can give huge advantage for the carriers. As the carriage is such an essential business not only for our commercial lives but also civil lives, the Commercial Act provides such a strong protection for the carriers.

However, we should note that there is an important exception for the rules described above. The Commercial Act Article 137(3) says, "Where the loss of, damage to or delay in delivery of goods has arisen from the willfulness or gross negligence of the carrier, he or she shall be liable for all damages." The Commercial Act does not protect a carrier who causes damages intentionally or with gross negligence. In that case, the civil law principles apply and the carrier shall have to compensate not only for usual damages, *i.e.* the price of the shoes, but also for unusual damages, i.e. the trading profit, if he had foreseen or could have foreseen the special circumstances.

On the other hand the Commercial Act Article 137(4) prevents the double gain by a carrier's client in calculating the amount of damages. It says, "Any freight charges and other expenses, the payment of which has been obviated by the loss of or damage to the goods, shall be deducted from the amount of the damages mentioned in the preceding three paragraphs."

D. Liability for Valuables

You recall that Rebecca sent a pair of high-end shoes worth KRW 1 million, and did not tell the carrier its price. The package was a valuable stuff and it could be a problem for her in claiming damages against the carrier that she concealed the price. The Commercial Act Article 136 says, "With respect to money, securities, or other valuables, the carrier shall be liable for damage only if the consignor has expressly stated the type and value thereof when consigning the transportation of the carriage." The special rule on valuables is designed to give the carrier an opportunity to pay special attention on the valuable goods and charge higher fee for the carriage.

General opinion says that a carrier does not have to compensate for damages at all, if the consignor did not expressly state the description and value of shipment. Moreover, a majority of commentators acknowledge the same result, even when the carrier neglected the care for ordinary goods.[103)] The reason is as follows: (i) it is hard to estimate the value of so-called "ordinary goods, and (ii) we need to promote the statement on valuables by the consignor.

However, the Commercial Act Article 136 shall not be applied, if a carrier intentionally causes the loss of or injury to the freight. Then which provision shall apply? A commentator says that the general principles under the Civil Act shall apply, which means that the carrier shall compensate not only for usual damages but also for unusual damages, if he had foreseen or could have foreseen the special circumstances.[104] Others say that the Commercial Act Article 137(1) and (2) shall apply, which means that the carrier need only to compensate for the price of the package.[105] My personal view is that the commercial law principles shall apply, as the other option seems a little too generous to the client who fraudulently conceal the price.

E. Conclusion

Now let us resolve the question presented in our case, by applying the above mentioned principles to the fact of case.

- According to the general opinion, the carrier does not have to compensate for the damages at all, as Madeline did not expressly state the value of shipment.
- According to a majority of commentators, the carrier still doesn't have to compensate for any damage, even if he neglected the care for ordinary goods.
- But if the carrier intentionally caused the injury to the freight, he shall have to compensate for the damages under the commercial law principles, which means that the carrier need only to compensate for the price of the package.

CHAPTER Ⅴ HOSPITALITY BUSINESS

Ⅰ. CONCEPT

The Commercial Act Article 151 gives us the definition of hospitality service provider (hereinafter "HSP"), in Korean *gong-joong-jop-gaek-op-ja*: "Any person who engages in the business of making transactions by theaters, hotels, restaurants, or other facilities used by the public is called a hospitality service provider" "Other facilities" here include public bathhouse, beauty parlor, billiard hall, golf course, *etc*. An HSP refers to a person who runs the business, not the owner of the facilities. Since the Commercial Act Article 46(9) lists "transactions by facilities used by the public" as basic commercial activities, an HSP is a merchant-by nature of business (Commercial Act Article 4).

Ⅱ. LIABILITIES OF AN HSP

[CASE] Chloe checked in a motel and parked her car in the parking lot across the street. The next morning she found the car stolen. But the operator of the motel denied any liability for her loss. Could Chloe claim damages against the operator? What if Chloe did not check in due to high price, and returned to the parking lot only to find her car damaged?

A. Issues

The case involves the issue of an HSP's liability for a deposited article. However, it's not evident whether the car was actually deposited to the operator, and it is a key point here whether the parking lot was under the motel operator's control. Before we resolve the case, let us first review the two types of liabilities of an HSP: (i) liabilities for a deposited article; and (ii) those for the personal belongings of guests.

B. Liability of an HSP for a Deposited Article

The Commercial Act Article 152(1) talks about the liability of an HSP for articles deposited from a guest. It says, "Unless a hospitality service provider proves that he or she has not been negligent in giving due care in the custody of articles deposited from his or her guests to him or her or his or her employee, the hospitality service provider shall be liable for damage resulting from the loss of or damage to the articles kept in his or her custody."

As was the case of a carrier, an HSP is liable for the damage to a deposited article, only when he or his performance assistant intentionally or negligently caused the damage. But again, so with the case of a carrier, the burden of proof shall be placed on the HSP.

The Commercial Act Article 152(1) applies only to the liability of HSP which is deposited from a guest. Thus an agreement to deposit an article is required here in order for an HSP to be liable for the damage. The agreement can either be express or tacit. If, for example, the parking lot has a locked gate or a keeper controls the access to the parking lot, an agreement for deposit could be implied. But if the motel simply provides the place for parking without controlling the access to the place, an agreement for deposit could be identified, only when the guest notify the motel of parking or entrusted the motel with the custody of the car by depositing a key.[106)]

"Guests" here refer to people who conclude a contract to use the facilities. However, a person who enters the place to use the facilities and is treated as a de facto guest shall also be included, even when she/he does not eventually conclude a contract to use the facilities. For example, guests here includes a person who fails to check in due to the lack of vacancy.

C. Liability of an HSP for the Personal Belongings of Guests

The Commercial Act Article 152(2) talks about the liability of an HSP for articles which are not deposited from a guest. It says, "A hospitality service provider shall be liable for damage for the loss of or damage to portable goods brought into his or her establishments, even if not particularly deposited by the guest, when it is due to the lack of due care of the business entity or any of his or her employees."

An HSP shall be liable for the damage to the personal belongings of a guest that are not deposited with the HSP, only when the guest proves the negligence of the HSP or her/his assistants. As those articles are under the control of the guest, not the HSP, the burden of proof is placed upon the guest.

D. Special Agreement for Exemption

During a vacation, when you checked in a hotel, you might have found a notice at the front desk or in your guest room that says, "The hotel is not liable for any loss or injury to the valuables that a guest does not deposit at the front desk." If the notice is valid, it is a bad new to the guests who did not deposit their jewelry at the front desk: they may not claim any damages against the operator, even when they can prove that it was caused by his negligence.

Fortunately for those guests, the Commercial Act Article 152(3) says, "No hospitality service provider shall be exonerated from liability under paragraphs (1) and (2), even if he or she has informed that he or she is not liable for the loss of or damage to the portable goods of guests." It means that a special agreement between an HSP and her/his guest to mitigate HSP's liability can be valid. However, an HSP may not be exempted from his liability by unilaterally notifying the guests that he shall not hold any liability for deposited articles or personal belongings of guests.

E. Conclusion

By applying those principles that we just reviewed to the fact of our case, we could resolve it as follows:

- If the parking lot is under the control of the motel, an agreement for deposit could be implied. Thus Chloe can claim damages against the motel, unless the motel proves that she or her assistant did not neglected care.
- If the parking lot is not under the control of the motel, a tacit agreement can be implied, when Chloe notified the motel of parking or entrusted with the custody of the car by depositing a key.
- Even if Chloe did not check in due to high price, she can claim damages against the motel as a de facto guest.
- The motel may not be exempt from the liability by unilaterally notifying Chloe that the motel shall not hold any liability.

ENDNOTES

1) *Business Laws In Korea: Investment, Taxation, and Industrial Property* (Chan-Jin Kim ed., 1982); Christine A. Genzberger *et al.*, *Korea Business: The Portable Encyclopedia for Doing Business with Korea* (1994); Igor Oleynik, *Korea South Business Law Handbook* (2006); Robert L. Brown, *Corporate Counsel's Guide to Doing Business in South Korea* (Allan S. Gutterman ed., 2010); Jasper S. Kim, *Korean Business Law: The Legal Landscape and Beyond* (2010).

2) *E.g.* Korean Legal Center, *Laws of the Republic of Korea* (1969).

3) International Business Publications, Inc., *Korea South Company Laws and Regulations Handbook Volume 1: Strategic Information and Basic Laws* (2015); Jong-Hoon Lee, *Corporation Laws & Cases of South Korea* (2016); Kyung-Hoon Chun *et al.*, *Corporations and Partnerships in South Korea* (3rd ed. 2019). *Korean Business Law* (Hwa-Jin Kim ed., 2012) also fosuses on selected issues in the areas of company law and capital market regulation.

4) Semin Park, *Insurance Law in South Korea* (2015); In Hyeon Kim, *Transport Law in South Korea* (3rd ed. 2017). *See also Mark Furse, Antitrust Law in China, Korea and Vietnam* (2009); Harry Hyungyu Lee, *Competition Law in Korea* (2015); *Intellectual Property Law in Korea* (Byung-Il Kim & Christopher Heath eds, 2d ed. 2015).

5) For more information on Korean legal system in general, *see* Korea Legislation Research Institute, *Introduction to Korean Law* (2012). For an introduction to Korean contract law, *see* Won-Lim Jee & Jung Won

Jun, *Contract Law in South Korea* (2019).

6) Joo-Chan Sohn, *Sang-Bop (Sang) [Commercial Law Volume I]* at 7 (14th ed. 2003); Dong-Yoon Chung, *Sang-Bop (Sang) [Commercial Law Volume I]* at 8 (6th ed. 2012); Wi-Doo Gang & Chae-Ho Lim, *Sang-Bop-Gang-Ui (Sang) [Lecture on Commercial Law Volome I]* at 5-6 (3rd ed. 2009). Some commentators define commercial law more narrowly as the special private law concerning business enterprises. Won-Sun Park, *Sae-Sang-Bop (Sang) [New Commercial Law Volume I]* at 36 (1962); Chan-Hyung Chung, *Sang-Bop-Gang-Ui (Sang) [Lecture on Commercial Law Volume I]* at 10-11 (20th ed. 2017); Chul-Song Lee, *Sang-Bop-Chong-Chik Sang-Haeng-Wi [General Principles of Commercial Law]* at 7-8 (14th ed. 2016); Junesun Choi, *Sang-Bop-Chong-Chik Sang-Haeng-Wi-Bop [General Principles of Commercial Law]* at 33 (10th ed. 2016); Sung-Tae Kim, S*ang-Bop -Chong-Chik Sang-Haeng-Wi-Bop Gang-Ron [Lecture on General Principles of Commercial Law]* at 19 (1998); Joong-Ho Lim, *Sang-Bop-Chong-Chik Sang-Haeng-Wi-Bop [General Principles of Commercial Law]* at 9-11 (2d ed. 2015). Others define commercial law as the law concerning merchants rather than business enterprises. Ki-Won Choi & Dong-Min Kim, *Sang-Bop-Hak-Sin-Ron (Sang) [The New Theory of Commercial Law Volume I]* at 5 (20th ed. 2014); Ki-Su Lee & Byeong-Gyu Choi, *Sang-Bop-Chong-Chik Sang-Haeng-Wi-Bop [General Principles of Commercial Law]* at 16-19 (8th ed. 2016).

7) Visit the website at *https://elaw.klri.re.kr/eng_service/main.do.*

8) For example, the current version of Commercial Act is Act No. 17362 amended on June 9, 2020. But the website provides the translation of an older version, Act No. 15755 amended on September 18, 2018. A

couple of years' delay seems inevitable in updating the website, considering the hardships of the project.

9) The Commercial Act Part II Chapter II (Sales) contains only 5 articles, while the Civil Act Part III Chapter II Section III (Sales) has 33 articles.

10) *See* the Civil Act Articles 580, 581, 572(2), (3) and 575(1).

11) *See* the Civil Act Article 582.

12) *See supra* Section Ⅱ.

13) *See infra* Part Ⅱ. Chapter Ⅰ. Section Ⅱ.

14) *See infra* Part Ⅱ. Chapter Ⅰ. Sectiou Ⅰ.

15) "Proviso," or *dan-so* in Korean, here means an article or clause that introduces a condition or exception. It typically starts with a clause, "Provided that … ."

16) *See* the Civil Act Part III Chapter I Section 3 Subsection 4 (Surety Obligation).

17) *See* the Civil Act Part II Chapter VIII (Pledge).

18) *See* the Civil Act Part II Chapter IX (Mortgage).

19) *See supra* Section Ⅱ.

20) The principle of the respect for outward appearance in Korean commercial law is in line with the *Rechisscheintheorie* in German law and the *estoppel by representation* in English law.

21) Joon-Ho Kim, *Min-Bop-Gang-Ui [Lecture on Civil Law]* at 506 (rev. ed. 1993).

22) Yoon-Jik Gwak, *Chae-Gwon-Chong-Ron [General Principles of the Law of Obligations]* at 249 (2d ed. 1981).

23) Soon-Han Gwon, *Min-Bop-Yo-Hae II: Chae-Gwon-Chong-Ron Gak-Ron [Lecture on Civil Law Volume II: The Law of Obligations]* at 358 (6th ed. 2011). E.g. Supreme Court of Korea, Decision of 20 August 1981, 80Da2587.

24) Supreme Court of Korea, Decision of 10 April 2014, 2013Da68207.

25) "IOU" here means an informal document acknowledging debt. We call it *"cha-yong-jung"* in Korean.

26) *See infra* Part Ⅲ. Chapter Ⅰ. Section Ⅲ. B.

27) *See* the Civil Act Part III Chapter II Section 13 (Partnership).

28) On the issuance of new shares after the establishment of a corporation, *see* the Commercial Act Part III Chapter IV Section 4.

29) *See* the Civil Act Part III Chapter II Section 5 (Loan for Consumption).

30) See the Commercial Act Part III Chapter IV Section 8 (Bonds).

31) *See infra* Part Ⅳ.

32) *See supra* Section Ⅰ.

33) *See infra* Part Ⅳ.

34) Joo-Chan Sohn, *supra* note 6, at 75.

35) Supreme Court of Korea, Decision of 13 April 2012, 2011Da104246.

36) Supreme Court of Korea, Decision of 26 July 2007, 2006Ma334.

37) *See supra* Part Ⅱ. Chapter Ⅱ. Section Ⅴ.

38) *See infra* Part Ⅳ.

39) Supreme Court of Korea, Decision of 23 August 1996, 95Da39472.

40) *See infra* Section Ⅲ. D.

41) Ki-Won Choi & Dong-Min Kim, *supra* note 6, at 89; Chan-Hyung Chung, *supra* note 6, at 103; Chul-Song Lee, *supra* note 6, at 145.

42) We call this type of legislative tactic *"joon-yong"* in Korean.

43) Joo-Chan Sohn, *supra* note 6, at 111; Dong-Yoon Chung, *supra* note 6, at 72; Chan-Hyung Chung, *supra* note 6, at 103; Chul-Song Lee, *supra* note 6, at 146; Junesun Choi, *supra* note 6, at 156; Ok-Ryol Song, *Sang-Bop-Gang-Ui [Lecture on Commercial Law]* at 42 (6th ed. 2016).

44) Joo-Chan Sohn, *supra* note 6, at 113; Ki-Won Choi & Dong-Min Kim, *supra* note 6, at 93; Ki-Su Lee & Byeong-Gyu Choi, *supra* note 6, at 164; Chan-Hyung Chung, *supra* note 6, at 196; Joong-Ho Lim, *supra* note 6, at 137; Junesun Choi, *supra* note 6, at 159; Ok-Ryol Song, *supra* note 32, at 45. Don-Gak Seo, *Sang-Bop-Gang-Ui (Sang) [Lecture on Commercial Law Volume I]* at 101 (3rd ed. 1990) asserts that a company here shall be confined to one which engages in the same kind of business as that of a principal merchant.

45) Supreme Court of Korea, Decision of 26 July 2007, 2006Ma334.

46) Supreme Court of Korea, Decision of 26 February 2002, 2001 Da73879.

47) Supreme Court of Korea, Decision of 28 April 1964, 63Da811.

48) Joo-Chan Sohn, *supra* note 6, at 139; Dong-Yoon Chung, *supra* note 6, at 81; Wi-Doo Gang & Jae-Ho Lim, *supra* note 6, at 95; Ki-Su Lee & Byeong-Gyu Choi, *supra* note 6, at 205; Chan-Hyung Chung, *supra* note 6, at 124; Ok-Ryol Song, *supra* note 32, at 53. On opposing views, *see* Chul-Song Lee, *supra* note 6, at 187; Junesun Choi, *supra* note 6, at 183.

49) Supreme Court of Korea, Decision of 26 March 2004, 2001Da72081.

50) Supreme Court of Korea, Decision of 27 December 2011, 2010Da 20754.

51) *See supra* Part Ⅱ. Chapter Ⅰ. Section Ⅴ. B.

52) Supreme Court of Korea, Decision of 31 March 1969, 68Da2270.

53) Supreme Court of Korea, Decision of 10 October 1989, 88Daka8354.

54) Supreme Court of Korea, Decision of 24 March 1987, 85Daka2219.

55) Supreme Court of Korea, Decision of 28 December 1982, 82Daka 887.

56) Supreme Court of Korea, Decision of 13 June 1978, 78Da236.

57) Joo-Chan Sohn, *supra* note 6, at 127; Ki-Won Choi & Dong-Min Kim, *supra* note 6, at 123; Wi-Doo Gang & Jae-Ho Lim, *supra* note 6, at 104; Chul-Song Lee, *supra* note 6, at 209-10.

58) Supreme Court of Korea, Decision of 24 March 1987, 85Daka2219. *See also* Dong-Yoon Chung, *supra* note 6, at 84-85; Ok-Ryol Song, *supra* note 32, at 62.

59) Ki-Won Choi & Dong-Min Kim, *supra* note 6, at 120; Chan-Hyung Chung, *supra* note 6, at 132-33; Joong-Ho Lim, *supra* note 6, at 181; Junesun Choi, *supra* note 6, at 175; Ok-Ryol Song, *supra* note 32, at 62. On an opposing view, *see* Chul-Song Lee, *supra* note 6, at 207.

60) Supreme Court of Korea, Decision of 26 July 1977, 77Da797.

61) Supreme Court of Korea, Decision of 12 November 1991, 91Da 18309. On an opposing view, *see* Wi-Doo Gang & Jae-Ho Lim, supra note 6, at 105-106.

62) Supreme Court of Korea, Decision of 13 April 2001, 2000Da10512.

63) Supreme Court of Korea, Decision of 22 March 1983, 82Daka1852.

64) Won-Sun Park, *supra* note 6, at 119; Hee-Chol Chung, *Sang-Bop-Hak (Sang) [A Study of Commercial Law Volume I]* at 119-120 (1990); Joo-Chan Sohn, *supra* note 6, at 172; Wi-Doo Gang & Jae-Ho Lim, *supra* note 6, at 128; Ki-Won Choi & Dong-Min Kim, *supra* note 6, at 148; Dong-Yoon Chung, *supra* note 6, at 99; Ki-Su Lee & Byeong Gyu Choi, *supra* note 6, at 234; Chan-Hyung Chung, *supra* note 6, at 156; Junesun Choi, *supra* note 6, at 206. *See also* Don-Gak Seo, *supra* note 33, at 129.

65) Supreme Court of Korea, Decision of 15 December 2008, 2007Ma 1154.

66) Honguine Rhim, *Sang-Bop-Chong-Chik [The General Provisions of the Commercial Act]* at 151-152 (1987); Chul-Song Lee, *supra* note 6, at 245; Joong-Ho Lim, *supra* note 6, at 213.

67) Supreme Court of Korea, Decision of 13 February 1979, 77Da2436.

68) Supreme Court of Korea, Decision of 29 October 1996, 96Da19321.

69) *See supra* Section Ⅲ.

70) Supreme Court of Korea, Decision of 17 December 1983, 83Daka 331.

71) Joo-Chan Sohn, *supra* note 6, at 189; Ki-Won Choi & Dong-Min Kim, *supra* note 6, at 164; Chan-Hyung Chung, *supra* note 6, at 166.

72) Dong-Yoon Chung, *supra* note 6, at 105; Chul-Song Lee, *supra* note 6, at 259; Joong-Ho Lim, *supra* note 6, at 237.

73) Chul-Song Lee, *supra* note 6, at 261-62; Ki-Won Choi & Dong-Min Kim, *supra* note 6, at 163.

74) Supreme Court of Korea, Decision of 24 July 2008, 2006Da24100; Joong-Ho Lim, *supra* note 6, at 238; Ok-Ryol Song, *supra* note 32, at 76.

75) Ki-Won Choi & Dong-Min Kim, *supra* note 6, at 164-65; Chul-Song Lee, *supra* note 6, at 263; Chan-Hyung Chung, *supra* note 6, at 167; Ok-Ryol Song, *supra* note 32, at 76. On opposing views, *see* Joo-Chan Sohn, *supra* note 6, at 189-90; Dong-Yoon Chung, *supra* note 6, at 105.

76) Supreme Court of Korea, Decision of 15 November 1977, 97Da 35085.

77) Supreme Court of Korea, Decision of 22 July 2005, 2005Da602.

78) Supreme Court of Korea, Decision of 29 March 2002, 2000Du8455.

79) Supreme Court of Korea, Decision of 8 October 1991, 91Da22018, 22025.

80) Supreme Court of Korea, Decision of 9 August 1981, 91Da15225.

81) Supreme Court of Korea, Decision of 28 June 1994, 93Da33173.

82) Supreme Court of Korea, Decision of 10 May 2012, 2011Da45217.

83) Supreme Court of Korea, Decision of 10 September 2015, 2014Da 80440.

84) Supreme Court of Korea, Decision of 26 December 1989, 88Daka 10128.

85) *Id.*

86) Supreme Court of Korea, Decision of 27 April 1976, 75Da1209.

87) Supreme Court of Korea, Decision of 11 April 2008, 2007da89722.

88) Joo-Chan Sohn, *supra* note 6, at 204; Chul-Song Lee, *supra* note 6, at 306.

89) *See* the Civil Act Part III Chapter II Section 11 (Mandate).

90) Supreme Court of Korea, Decision of 22 April 2003, 2000Da55775, 55782.

91) *See supra* Section Ⅱ. A. 1.

92) *See supra* Part Ⅱ. Chapter Ⅱ. Section Ⅳ. B.

93) Ki-Won Choi & Dong-Min Kim, *supra* note 6, at 258; Ki-Su Lee & Byeong Gyu Choi, *supra* note 6, at 396; Chul-Song Lee, *supra* note 6, at 466; Chan-Hyung Chung, *supra* note 6, at 295; Junesun Choi, *supra* note 6, at 323; Ok-Ryol Song, *supra* note 32, at 149. On opposing views, *see* Joo-Chan Sohn, *supra* note 6, at 293; Wi-Doo Gang & Jae-Ho Lim, *supra* note 6, at 240.

94) *See supra* Part Ⅱ. Chapter Ⅰ. Section Ⅳ.

95) On a brief discussion of those views, *see* Ki Jong Lee, *Sang-Bop [Commercial Law]* at 131 (2d ed. 2020).

96) *See supra* Section Ⅰ. A.

97) *See infra* Section Ⅲ. D.

98) *See infra* Chapter Ⅰ. Section Ⅱ. B.

99) *See infra* Par Ⅱ. Chapter Ⅰ. Section Ⅰ.

100) *See infra* Chapter Ⅰ. Section Ⅲ. A.

101) Supreme Court of Korea, Decision of 26 April 1983, 82Nu92.

102) *See* the Civil Act Part III Chapter II Section 9 (Contract for Work).

103) Wi-Doo Gang & Jae-Ho Lim, *supra* note 6, at 283; Ki-Won Choi & Dong-Min Kim, *supra* note 6, at 354; Chan-Hyung Chung, *supra* note 6, at 356. On an opposing view, *see* Chul-Song Lee, *supra* note 6, at 533-34.

104) Chul-Song Lee, *supra* note 6, at 535.

105) Chan-Hyung Chung, *supra* note 6, at 356; Ki-Su Lee & Byeong Gyu Choi, *supra* note 6, at 478.

106) Supreme Court of Korea, Decision of 11 February 1992, 91Da 21800.

REFERENCES

Brown, Robert L., *Corporate Counsel's Guide to Doing Business in South Korea* (Allan S. Gutterman ed., 2010).

Choi, Junesun, *Sang-Bop-Chong-Chik Sang-Haeng-Wi-Bop [General Principles of Commercial Law]* (10th ed. 2016).

Choi, Ki-Won, & Dong-Min Kim, *Sang-Bop-Hak-Sin-Ron (Sang) [The New Theory of Commercial Law Volume I]* (20th ed. 2014).

Chun, Kyung-Hoon, *et al.*, *Corporations and Partnerships in South Korea* (3rd ed. 2019).

Chung, Chan-Hyung, *Sang-Bop-Gang-Ui (Sang) [Lecture on Commercial Law Volume I]* (20th ed. 2017).

Chung, Dong-Yoon, *Sang-Bop (Sang) [Commercial Law Volume I]* (6th ed. 2012).

Chung, Hee-Chol, *Sang-Bop-Hak (Sang) [A Study of Commercial Law Volume I]* (1990).

Furse, Mark, *Antitrust Law in China, Korea and Vietnam* (2009).

Gang, Wi-Doo, & Chae-Ho Lim, *Sang-Bop-Gang-Ui (Sang) [Lecture on Commercial Law Volome I]* (3rd ed. 2009).

Genzberger, Christine A., et al., *Korea Business: The Portable Encyclopedia for Doing Business with Korea* (1994).

Gwak, Yoon-Jik, *Chae-Gwon-Chong-Ron [General Principles of the Law of Obligations]* (2d ed. 1981).

Gwon, Soon-Han, *Min-Bop-Yo-Hae II: Chae-Gwon-Chong-Ron Gak-Ron*

[Lecture on Civil Law Volume II: The Law of Obligations] (6th ed. 2011).

International Business Publications, Inc., *Korea South Company Laws and Regulations Handbook Volume 1: Strategic Information and Basic Laws* (2015).

Jee, Won-Lim, & Jung Won Jun, *Contract Law in South Korea* (2019).

Kim, Byung-Il, & Christopher Heath eds., *Intellectual Property Law in Korea* (2d ed. 2015).

Kim, Chan-Jin, ed., *Business Laws In Korea: Investment, Taxation, and Industrial Property* (1982).

Kim, Hwa-Jin, ed., *Korean Business Law* (2012).

Kim, In Hyeon, *Transport Law in South Korea* (3rd ed. 2017).

Kim, Jasper S., *Korean Business Law: The Legal Landscape and Beyond* (2010).

Kim, Joon-Ho, *Min-Bop-Gang-Ui [Lecture on Civil Law]* (rev. ed. 1993).

Kim, Sung-Tae, *Sang-Bop-Chong-Chik Sang-Haeng-Wi-Bop Gang-Ron [Lecture on General Principles of Commercial Law]* (1998).

Korea Legislation Research Institute, *Introduction to Korean Law* (2012).

Korean Legal Center, *Laws of the Republic of Korea* (1969).

Lee, Chul-Song, *Sang-Bop-Chong-Chik Sang-Haeng-Wi [General Principles of Commercial Law]* (14th ed. 2016).

Lee, Harry Hyungyu, *Competition Law in Korea* (2015).

Lee, Jong-Hoon, *Corporation Laws & Cases of South Korea* (2016).

Lee, Ki Jong, *Sang-Bop [Commercial Law]* (2d ed. 2020).

Lee, Ki-Su, & Byeong-Gyu Choi, *Sang-Bop-Chong-Chik Sang-Haeng-Wi-Bop [General Principles of Commercial Law]* (8th ed. 2016).

Lim, Joong-Ho, *Sang-Bop-Chong-Chik Sang-Haeng-Wi-Bop [General Principles of Commercial Law]* (2d ed. 2015).

Oleynik, Igor, *Korea South Business Law Handbook* (2006).

Park, Semin, *Insurance Law in South Korea* (2015).

Park, Won-Sun, *Sae-Sang-Bop (Sang) [New Commercial Law Volume I]* (1962).

Rhim, Honguine, *Sang-Bop-Chong-Chik [The General Provisions of the Commercial Act]* (1987).

Seo, Don-Gak, *Sang-Bop-Gang-Ui (Sang) [Lecture on Commercial Law Volume I]* (3rd ed. 1990).

Sohn, Joo-Chan, *Sang-Bop (Sang) [Commercial Law Volume I]* (14th ed. 2003).

Song, Ok-Ryol, *Sang-Bop-Gang-Ui [Lecture on Commercial Law]* (6th ed. 2016).

INDEX

[A]

[B]

[C]

[F]

[G]

[H]

[I]

[J]

[L]

[P]

[R]